# The Cambridge Line

Even Liverpool Street
could look romantic

# The Cambridge Line

## Michael R. Bonavia MA, PhD, FCIT

ELY NORTH

63610

Ian ALLAN Publishing

First published 1995

ISBN 0 7110 2333 6

Published by Ian Allan Publishing

an imprint of Ian Allan Ltd, Terminal House, Station Approach, Shepperton, Surrey TW17 8AS.
Printed by Ian Allan Printing Ltd, Coombelands House, Coombelands Lane, Addlestone, Weybridge, Surrey KT15 1HY.

*Cover photos by R. C. Riley (front and back cover top) and Brian Morrison (back cover bottom).*

# Contents

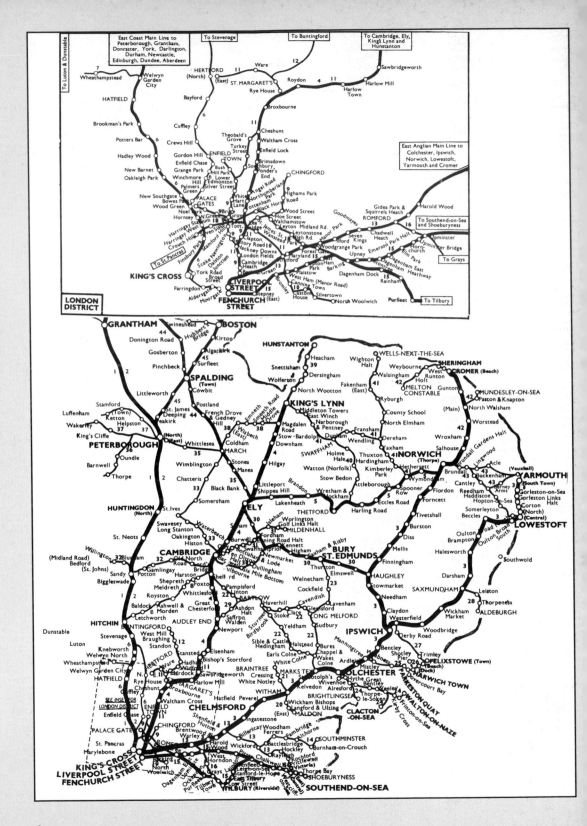

# The Cambridge Line

# Introduction

I have been fortunate to know the Cambridge line at various periods of my life. First, as an undergraduate, I spent many hours on station platforms which I fear ought to have been spent in a library or lecture room. Then, I commuted daily from the Buntingford branch to London for three years. Later, as head of the Eastern Region Planning Office, I was involved in the electrification to Bishop's Stortford. Still later, for a year I commuted daily from Cambridge to BR Headquarters in London. And even after I retired, family matters often took me to Cambridge.

I recall countless journeys, including inspecting the line from the comfort of the General Manager's saloon, to rough riding on the footplate of a 'Sandringham' in steam days, and the smoother experiences in the cab of a Class 37 diesel and the front end of a Stansted Express electric. I knew those two stalwart characters, Charlie and Arthur, who staffed an RBK on fixed turn, and fed the passengers between 'The Street' and King's Lynn over so many years. I can truly say that the Cambridge line has been part of my life.

*M.R.B.*

## Acknowledgements

Many people, over many years, from top management at Liverpool Street to porter-signalmen at branch line stations, have helped me with reminiscences of the Cambridge line. So far as written records are concerned, there is a debt owing to the always helpful staff in the Public Record Office at Kew and the Local History Librarians, above all in the Cambridgeshire Collection. Secondary material has of course included Cecil J. Allen's *The Great Eastern Railway*, the volume on East Anglia in the 'Regional Railway Histories of Great Britain' series and numerous shorter histories of individual branches such as P. Paye's *The Buntingford Branch*.

And, short though they are, the late Canon R.B. Fellows's two classic monographs, *London to Cambridge by Train, 1845-1938* and *Railways to Cambridge, Actual and Proposed* must never be overlooked.

Those who have read portions of my text and commented helpfully have included that renowned railway author-cum-senior manager, R.H.N. Hardy. But a very special debt is owed to Lyn D. Brooks, GER Locomotive Information Coordinator of the Great Eastern Railway Society, who devoted much time and trouble to helping me with Chapter 7. His erudition much improved my text, though any remaining errors are my sole responsibility.

An outline sketch of Bishopsgate station frontage, as in GER days. *British Rail*

7

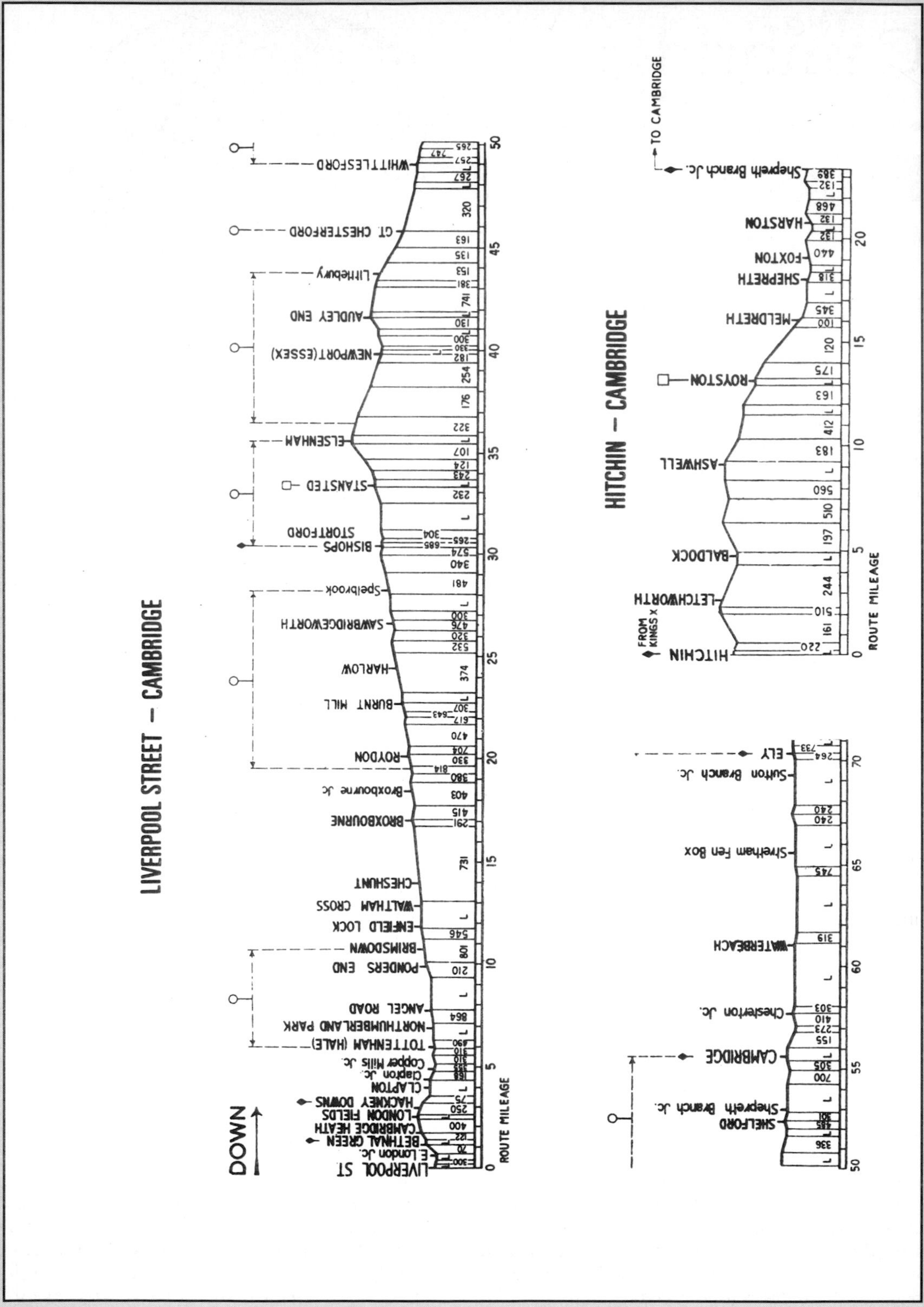

LIVERPOOL STREET – CAMBRIDGE
DOWN
LIVERPOOL ST
E. London Jc.
BETHNAL GREEN
CAMBRIDGE HEATH
LONDON FIELDS
HACKNEY DOWNS
CLAPTON
Clapton Jc.
Copper Mills Jc.
TOTTENHAM (HALE)
NORTHUMBERLAND PARK
ANGEL ROAD
PONDERS END
BRIMSDOWN
ENFIELD LOCK
WALTHAM CROSS
CHESHUNT
BROXBOURNE
Broxbourne Jc.
ROYDON
BURNT MILL
HARLOW
SAWBRIDGEWORTH
Spelbrook
BISHOPS STORTFORD
STANSTED
ELSENHAM
NEWPORT (ESSEX)
AUDLEY END
Littlebury
GT. CHESTERFORD
WHITTLESFORD
ROUTE MILEAGE
HITCHIN – CAMBRIDGE
HITCHIN
FROM KINGS X
LETCHWORTH
BALDOCK
ASHWELL
ROYSTON
MELDRETH
SHEPRETH
FOXTON
HARSTON
Shepreth Branch Jc.
TO CAMBRIDGE
ROUTE MILEAGE
SHELFORD
Shepreth Branch Jc.
CAMBRIDGE
Chesterton Jc.
WATERBEACH
Stretham Fen Box
Sutton Branch Jc.
ELY

# By Cambridge to York:
# Visions and Harsh Reality

Cambridge in the 1830s was not only the seat of one of the two oldest English universities but also a busy market town in the centre of an important agricultural area, sited about 55 miles from central London on an axis only slightly east of due north. It thus would seem to be a natural staging point for a railway from London to York and the North-East, particularly since the terrain between London and Cambridge offers few difficulties from an engineering point of view. The Lea (or Lee) Valley (both spellings are in use) runs conveniently north and south between Stratford and just beyond Broxbourne, a level route for 16 miles. Thereafter there is gently undulating ground, intersected as far as Bishop's Stortford by the valley of the canalised River Stort. Beyond comes the slightly more hilly territory rather grandly known as the East Anglian Heights, actually the gentler end of the Chilterns. Nothing to frighten a railway engineer!

Accordingly, starting in 1825, three railway lines were surveyed, either in detail or by a simple view of the country. The first was proposed by the brothers John and George Rennie, both experienced engineers, under the title of The Northern Rail-Road Company. The route they chose from London to Cambridge was not the easiest but the most direct since it ran via Hoddesdon, Ware, Braughing and Barkway, disdaining the use of the river valleys and cutting through the higher ground. Beyond Cambridge everything was left vague. A proposal to deposit a bill in Parliament was advertised and it was stated that the ultimate object was to extend the line to Cromford in Derbyshire and join the High Peak Railway, that steeply-graded mineral line, so as to reach Manchester. The scheme collapsed (deservedly, one may think) for want of public support.

The next proposal was put forward by the well-known canal engineer, Nicholas Wilcox Cundy. As one would expect from his previous background, Cundy favoured a level route, taking advantage of watercourses such as the Lea and the Stort.

Cundy's line ran to Bishop's Stortford, thence to Cambridge; it was intended to reach York later, with a branch from somewhere south of Cambridge to Norwich. The imposing title of the whole project was the Grand North-Eastern Railway. The only detailed plans drawn were for the London to Cambridge section. The railway failed however to take shape as a company, even though preliminary steps for a Parliamentary bill were taken in 1834.

A bill was actually deposited for a third line between London and Cambridge surveyed by Joseph Gibbs. This took a more easterly course and passed through higher ground via Dunmow and Saffron Walden in Essex. It also was intended to reach York eventually and to have a branch from south of Cambridge to Norwich. Its title was The Great Northern Railway — nothing to do with its illustrious successor of that name.

With these three schemes on the table, a committee 'for promoting a railway from London to York, with a branch to Norwich' was formed and it invited James Walker FRS to report on the merits or otherwise of the three proposals. Walker came down conclusively in favour of Cundy's route, and a bill for a Northern & Eastern Railway, departing only slightly from Cundy's line, was deposited in 1830. A rival bill for a Great Northern Railway based on Gibbs's route was also deposited but failed to obtain a Second Reading. Nor did the Northern & Eastern bill, though passed, escape without severe amendment. It was perhaps lucky to survive at all,

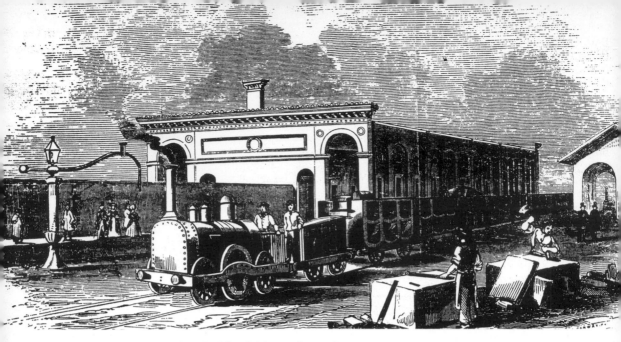

An old print, often reproduced, of Cambridge station as built. (There was probably some artistic licence in the drawing.) *Author's Collection*

thanks partly to the University. Even so, it abandoned the idea of reaching York and only included beyond Cambridge a line to Newmarket, Thetford, Norwich and Yarmouth. Sadly, Parliament cut down the Northern and Eastern to a London-Cambridge line about 53 miles long starting from a terminus at Islington, reaching Tottenham (Ferry Lane) and the Lea Valley by a tunnel under the Clapton terrace.

Planning of the London end seems to have been ill-conceived. Islington was inconveniently far from central London, and the cost of tunnelling through the high ground excessive.

In any case, subscriptions to the capital issue came in slowly. Robert Stephenson was originally appointed consulting engineer for the construction of the line, but he had many more important projects to supervise and was soon joined by Joseph Braithwaite, who was already responsible for the Eastern Counties Railway. Braithwaite eventually took over the main responsibility.

The shortage of money forced the company to take the unwelcome step of postponing any extension beyond Bishop's Stortford on the one hand, and — very sensibly — seeking a cheaper route into London. A first thought was to divert the line from Tottenham through Plaistow and Stratford to join the London & Blackwall Railway,

using the latter's forthcoming terminus in Fenchurch Street. That was quickly replaced by a simpler solution, namely to continue down the Lea Valley to Stratford and join the Eastern Counties Railway, sharing its Shoreditch terminus (later called Bishopsgate) in London. Parliamentary powers for this diversion were obtained in 1839, and in 1840 abandonment for the time being of the Bishop's Stortford–Cambridge section was also authorised.

Getting into London was not as easy as had been hoped. The Eastern Counties Railway at first refused to co-operate; then feeling the financial pinch itself, relented and agreed to admit the Northern & Eastern into Shoreditch via Stratford in return for a rent of £7,000 per annum for 20 years, plus a toll of four pence per passenger and other tolls on freight.

The appointment of Braithwaite and the sharing of ECR facilities made it necessary for the Northern & Eastern to adopt the rather eccentric 5ft gauge sponsored by Braithwaite and adopted by the Eastern Counties.

Considering the exceptionally easy nature of the terrain, construction seems to have been desperately slow, mainly due to shortage of money. It took some four years after passage of the bill, until September 1840, for the rails to reach Broxbourne, just over 15 miles from Stratford. This was despite the fact that earthworks were negligible and most road crossings were on the level: the only gradient of any significance was a short stretch of 1 in 210 at Ponder's

End. Harlow was reached in August 1841 and Bishop's Stortford in May 1842.

Meanwhile, the Northern & Eastern had felt threatened by a revival of interest in the Rennie route through Ware to Cambridge. It countered this by obtaining powers for a short branch from just north of Broxbourne to Ware and Hertford — again cheap to construct, beside the water meadows of the River Lea. This useful branch was opened in October 1843. Its additional traffic receipts may have heartened the Board of the Northern & Eastern to obtain the powers needed to continue from Bishop's Stortford to Newport (Essex), only 16 miles short of the ultimate objective, Cambridge.

Simultaneously, discussions had been taking place with the Board of the Eastern Counties regarding a merger, obviously a sensible move. These were successful and on 1 January 1844 the ECR took over the working of the Northern & Eastern by agreeing to pay 5% per annum on the latter's capital expenditure up to a maximum of £970,000, plus a division of surplus profits.

During its short life as a working railway (the Company continued to exist in 'shell' form until 1902) the Northern & Eastern had not been well regarded by the public. The historian of Tottenham's railways says that the directors adopted a 'take it or leave it' attitude to the public; certainly, even the shareholders became restive and set up a Committee of Inquiry which resulted in a drastic shake-out of the Board. It was not only Directors who were removed; Braithwaite's appointment was ended in 1843. John Braithwaite was originally more of a mechanical than a civil engineer (the distinction was not clear-cut at that date — witness the activities of the Stephensons and Brunel, for example). He had worked on the *Novelty* for the Rainhill trials and was a partner in the locomotive building firm of Braithwaite & Milner which supplied locomotives to the Eastern Counties and the Northern & Eastern.

Braithwaite is chiefly remembered for his curious advocacy of a 5ft gauge for the Eastern Counties and hence the Northern & Eastern. The Eastern Counties had toyed with the idea of following Brunel and adopting the 7ft broad gauge: Braithwaite agreed that something a little wider than the Stephenson gauge of 4ft 8 $\frac{1}{2}$in would produce 'a more quiet action of the water in the boiler and consequently less ebullition'! But, to do him justice, he solved successfully a difficult civil engineering task in carrying the railway across the marshes in the lower Lea Valley by pile-driving and spoil-tipping.

An old print of Queen Victoria's arrival at a specially reconstructed pavilion at Tottenham station; this platform was provided for her journey to Cambridge with Prince Albert who was being installed as Chancellor of the University on 5 July 1847. *Author's Collection*

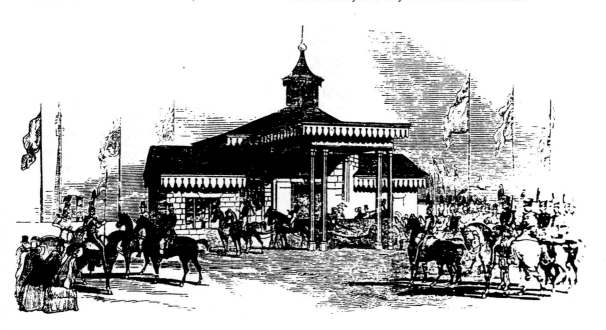

The original Northern & Eastern trains were slow and the carriages cheaply built, though painted blue until 1844 – an unusual colour for the times. The best locomotives used were probably the Stephenson 2-2-2 type with 'haycock', or 'Gothic' fireboxes, though one of the Stephenson 'long boiler' engines was supplied by that firm in 1841. Bury 2-2-0 locos, with bar frames, which were built by Braithwaite & Milner, were almost certainly in use as well.

By and large, the place of the Northern & Eastern in our railway history is not a distinguished one. Certainly it did not provide an appropriate first link in a chain of lines adequate to comprise a great trunk route from London to the North. It was cheaply built, with a number of timber bridges. The chief contractor, Samuel Morton Peto, did not set such high standards as Thomas Brassey or William Cubitt. Keen to get contracts, he often accepted at least part payment in the shares of his client company, and would cut costs if necessary. The Northern & Eastern, in fact, was built to a restrictive loading gauge that was to prove a nuisance later on in some locations. After the merger with the Eastern Counties things began to improve somewhat, though not enough to satisfy the shareholders by any means.

Old print (1856) of the original starting-point of the Northern & Eastern Railway, the junction with the Eastern Counties Railway. Architect Francis Thompson.
*Author's Collection*

Great Chesterford station, Eastern Counties Railway, was designed by the architect Francis Thompson.
*Author's Collection*

# The Eastern Counties Take-Over

Whether the Eastern Counties obtained a good bargain from the merger terms with the Northern & Eastern is arguable. The ECR was — and for a long time remained — in financial difficulties. An early Victorian Cockney ballad sang of

'. . . the Eastern Counties Railway
Vich the shares I don't desire'

and its difficulty in raising capital was reflected in the painful slowness of its progress towards its main traffic objective, Norwich via Ipswich. It had obtained its Act of Parliament on the same day as the Northern & Eastern, 4 July 1836. It opened from Devonshire Street in London's East End to Romford in June 1839; from Devonshire Street to Shoreditch, and from Romford to Brentwood, in July 1840. It finally staggered, exhausted, into Colchester in March 1843. Powers to extend further had by then lapsed and had to be renewed, but by another company, the Eastern Union, formed to link Colchester with Ipswich, and promoted by local interests disillusioned with the Eastern Counties.

Though stuck at Colchester, the Eastern Counties did manage to revive the activities on the Cambridge line, by getting powers to extend from Newport (Essex) through Cambridge and Ely to Brandon. Why Brandon? The reason for the switch of interest and development away from a potential trunk line to the North was the energy of the citizens of Norwich who, like many at Ipswich, were disappointed by the snail-like progress of the ECR. They first of all successfully promoted a short local railway from Norwich to Yarmouth, which opened in 1844, and in the same year obtained parliamentary powers for a Norwich & Brandon Railway to join the Eastern Counties at the latter town.

The Norwich & Brandon railway amalgamated with the Norwich & Yarmouth in 1844 and the combined undertaking took the title of the Norfolk Railway. The line to Brandon was through easy country for most of the way, with few gradients of any significance. It was opened in July 1845, and the opening ceremony also celebrated the completion of the former Northern & Eastern line from Newport (Essex) through Cambridge and Ely to Brandon. The junketings, with trains from London and Norwich meeting, were focused on a visit to Ely Cathedral and a huge banquet at Cambridge. The speeches on this occasion included one from the Dean of Ely in which he addressed the contractor, Peto, who was a well-known dissenter, and urged him to recognise the 'advantage and blessing' of becoming a member of the Church of England!

The Cambridge main line thus started as a London-Norwich route, but all the time there was the shadow of the alternative route via Colchester, significantly shorter, coming to completion. When this took place, the principal traffic through Cambridge from London might have to be to the north rather than the east.

Northward from Ely the line was built by the Lynn & Ely Railway. A branch to Wisbech was included. Powers for the work were obtained in June 1845 and the line opened in October 1847. Crossing fenland and the main waterways of the Bedford Level Corporation were the main problems. Even today the character of the subsoil imposes speed limits on trains here.

The Cambridge main line thus from 1847 divided at Ely, which became an important junction. However, Cambridge may be considered as the primary traffic objective from London. The first train service to the university town comprised seven down and six up trains. (One wonders how the rolling stock position was balanced!) One train each way was described as a 'quick train', taking 1hr 50min over the journey in the down direction and 2hr in the up direction. Extra fares were charged for the 'quickness' of 31.2mph down and 28.6mph up. Only one train in each direction carried third class passengers and it took around 4hr, travelling at little more than the speed of a mail coach.

There was however a short period only five years after the opening when Norwich trains via Cambridge offered some of the fastest running in England. The 5pm from Shoreditch (renamed Bishopsgate) in 1850 ran non-stop to Cambridge with an average speed of about 43mph, and continued with speeds of 42mph to Ely and 48mph, astonishing for that date, from Ely to Wymondham. It reached Norwich in 3hr 15min.

Sadly, this enterprise was not to be long-lived. Two years later a Bishop's Stortford stop was added and timings were extended; after 1855 there was a general deceleration.

Before all this could take place, it had been necessary for both the Eastern Counties and the Northern & Eastern to adopt the standard gauge in place of Braithwaite's eccentric 5ft gauge. The changeover was not opposed by Braithwaite when Robert Stephenson reported that it would

*Above:* A scene at Cambridge in 1870 with Sinclair 2-2-2 No 88, built by Schneider of Creusot, apparently heading a special train in the station yard. *National Railway Museum/Crown Copyright Reserved*

*Below:* One of the goods engines used on the Cambridge line and known as 'Ironclads' — a 4-4-0 designed by W. Adams, built 1877. *National Railway Museum/Crown Copyright Reserved*

be advisable, and it was carried out under Stephenson's supervision in under five weeks, a very effective operation. For some reason — perhaps just to impress the public with the change of management from Northern & Eastern to Eastern Counties — at the same time the blue livery of the coaches and the blue liveries of the N & E staff were changed to green. An early example of the desire for a corporate image!

The London and Cambridge line had some structures of interest. In London it shared Shoreditch (Bishopsgate) terminus with the Colchester line trains. The original skimpy station erected by the ECR in 1840 had to be enlarged and improved in 1848/49, largely to provide for the Cambridge line trains. The full story of Shoreditch/Bishopsgate is covered in Chapter 8.

Other stations were cheaply built and had to be renewed and improved; Tottenham was rebuilt in 1859 after many complaints about the inadequacy of the original station. There were some exceptions to the general rule of cheapness and nastiness; surprisingly, the Eastern Counties, despite its poverty, did not begrudge paying fees to architects of standing such as Francis Thompson and Sancton Wood, and a few stations on the Northern and Eastern were attractive – for instance Roydon, built in 1841 in wood, with a charming bow-fronted verandah. Bishop's Stortford had a solid block of station offices which was a nicely balanced composition.

Further north, and built by the Eastern Counties, came Audley End, originally named Wenden after the hamlet nearby (later Wendens Ambo). The grander title for the station derives from the great mansion owned by Lord Braybrooke in the vicinity. Audley End (Wenden) station, dating from 1845, was designed by Francis Thompson and survives today, listed grade II. It has classical proportions and a dignified *porte-cochère*, no doubt included mainly for the benefit of Lord Braybrooke, his family and guests using the station.

Just north of the station are two short tunnels which have a rather splendid portal with the Braybrooke arms displayed — something insisted upon when the land was conveyed to the railway company by his Lordship.

Nearer to Cambridge is Great Chesterford station, very similar to Audley End, by the same architect and built at the same time. It differs only in details.

Lastly, Cambridge's unusual station was built in 1845. Its history is covered in Chapter 6.

Having struggled to Norwich, the Eastern Counties was about to be galvanised into activity by a sort of earthquake — the arrival of George Hudson, the 'Railway King', as its Chairman. The shareholders of the Eastern Counties were thoroughly dissatisfied with the company's direction and management; the first half-year's dividend in 1845 had been a miserable 1%. During the summer of that year approaches were made to Hudson, who seemed to have the magic art of creating dividends out of thin air, to assume the Chairmanship, which he did from 30 October 1845. The shareholders greeted his first appearance, according to the *Railway Times*, 'with a loud and long-continued burst of cheering'.

They did not realise that Hudson was using the ECR as a pawn in his game of opposing the scheme for a direct railway from London to York by using the Cambridge and Ely line built by the

The implication of this warning notice (location not identified) suggests off-duty rambling habits among staff! *GER Society*

This even more bizarre notice seems to suggest that railwaymen bring their families train-spotting in their spare time! *GER Society*

Northern and Eastern and the Eastern Counties. Hudson's 'empire' largely consisted of a chain of railways linking York and the North-East with London via Derby, Leicester and Rugby, where the London & Birmingham was joined. This circuitous route was threatened by the natural demand for a more direct railway which led to surveys being made for two lines, the 'Direct Northern' and the 'London & York', the latter supported by that remarkable and pugnacious Yorkshireman Edmund Denison. Hudson's plan was to forestall the London & York scheme by extending the Eastern Counties to March, Spalding, Lincoln and Doncaster. The capital for this grandiose scheme was to be raised by the issue of 'Eastern Counties Extension Shares'. The total cost of this alternative London to York railway, after incorporating the Eastern Counties, was to be about £4 ½ million. However, the scheme collapsed when the Direct Northern and London & York interests joined forces and their bill, based on the London & York's route, was passed in June 1845.

Hudson soon started 'fiddling the books' of the Eastern Counties, though the initial euphoria at the higher dividends he declared had enabled him to get approval for extensions designed to combat the London & York – from Ely to March and Peterborough, for instance, opened in March 1847.

Meanwhile, he had declared a dividend in January 1846 that was three times as high as anything paid before. Needless to say, it had not been earned. But he pushed the capital expenditure of the Eastern Counties from £3,804,000 when he assumed the Chairmanship to £13,139,000 by the beginning of 1849. Much of this went in paying guaranteed dividends to leased or extension undertakings, and dividends to ECR ordinary shareholders. The crash was bound to come and in 1849 Hudson, with a Committee of Enquiry uncovering numerous instances of fiddling the ECR accounts, resigned.

The dream of a trunk line to the North through Cambridge went into suspense, and it was not to be revived until the Great Northern Railway had come into being; and even then the contest was to be over Yorkshire coal for London, not express trains to York. The Eastern Counties meanwhile completed its route to Norwich via Colchester by buying up the Eastern Union, which had filled in the gap from Ipswich to Colchester, in 1854 and thereby had a route some 11 miles shorter from London to Norwich than the line through Cambridge. However, even up to modern times, a proportion of Norwich trains continued to be routed via Cambridge.

# The Newmarket Railway: a Short, Sad Tale

Just 110 years before Dr Beeching was appointed to reorganise British Railways, a closure of which he would no doubt have approved took place — that of the short–lived Newmarket & Chesterford Railway, which for a time seemed to offer the prospect of becoming quite an important trunk line and an alternative London to Norwich route scarcely longer than that via Colchester. It threatened to side-track Cambridge.

In July 1846 a company was incorporated to build a line from Great Chesterford on the Bishop's Stortford-Cambridge section of the Eastern Counties to Newmarket, with a branch to Cambridge from Six Mile Bottom. The Jockey Club of Newmarket favoured the proposal, which gave the racing fraternity the prospect of a better rail service to London than that which could be obtained via Cambridge. It was said that MPs could have a day's racing and attend a debate in the same evening — clearly an important advantage.

The total length of the line was 17 ½ miles. It was opened in April 1848 for passenger trains, with six locomotives, 88 coaches and — significantly — 40 horse boxes and carriage trucks.

This little railway had strategic importance, since it could, if extended from Newmarket to Thetford, offer an alternative route to Norwich. Bury St Edmunds was another possible destination. There was, therefore, competition between the Eastern Counties and the Norfolk Railway prior to the absorption of the latter by the former in 1848, for control of the Newmarket line while this was still under construction. After its opening, although relations were difficult, the ECR did run some through trains to Newmarket from Shoreditch, in 2hr 20min by the quickest train.

The finances of the little railway were doubtful from the start, partly because its construction had involved traversing the East Anglian Heights, with some quite substantial cuttings and embankments. Its main hope had to lie in selling itself as a component of a new trunk route, an alternative to that through Cambridge. But the absorption of the Norfolk Railway by the ECR closed this option.

The Newmarket Company tried another expedient, approaching the Great Northern Railway with the idea of an extension from Great Chesterford to Royston, but this also failed. Then the Newmarket directors thought they had managed to unload upon the Eastern Counties, but this depended upon an agreement that the Eastern Counties shareholders refused to confirm. There followed a short period during which the Eastern Counties worked the railway on a basis very unsatisfactory to the unfortunate Newmarket shareholders and in June 1850 the Great Chesterford–Newmarket line was closed.

However, a new Chairman, Cecil Fane, and a new Manager, G.W. Brown, infused fresh life into the concern. With rolling stock borrowed from the ECR, the Chesterford–Newmarket line was reopened and some much needed revenue began to flow in. The new management was skilful enough to persuade the debenture holders to accept a conversion of the interest rate from 5% to 3 ½%, and the contractor to reduce his outstanding claim by £26,000. It even negotiated a fresh agreement with the Eastern Counties giving a partial guarantee of a dividend on the Newmarket shares.

Dreams of reaching Thetford (for Norwich) or of extending to Bury St Edmunds having been abandoned, all energies were now concentrated upon getting the Cambridge–Newmarket route completed as quickly as possible. Fortunately it ran through more level country than the Great

*Left:* Six Mile Bottom station was the point where the direct Newmarket line would have joined the eventual route via Cambridge. *Author's Collection*

*Left:* Audley End station pictured on an unknown date; the entire staff are on parade for the photograph — including the shunting horse on the up line. *T. Middlemass*

Chesterford–Six Mile Bottom stretch, though it ended in a notorious eight-chain radius curve just north of Cambridge, where wheel flanges squealed their protest until the GER realigned the curve in 1896. The contractor's bill for the work was reduced by singling the track between Great Chesterford and Six Mile Bottom and using the recovered materials on the Cambridge section. The line was opened in October 1851, and this was followed by the Company's first dividend payment. Anticipating Dr Beeching's tactics, the singling of the track of the former direct Newmarket line was to be followed by closure, with the Eastern Counties taking over both lines. Complete abandonment of the Great Chesterford–Six Mile Bottom section however needed Parliamentary sanction, not given until 1858.

Had the closure taken place more recently the track might have been converted into a pleasant path for walkers, some seven miles long. Day tickets, out to Great Chesterford and returning from Six Mile Bottom via Cambridge, would have been quite an attractive proposition for ramblers' clubs. Sadly, however, the Newmarket Railway has almost vanished with few traces of earthworks, apart from those in the Pampisford area; only one or two bridges remain to puzzle visitors as to their significance. Few will realise that expresses to Norwich might have passed this way, had the railway politics of the 1840s been different.

As a postscript, it should be mentioned that in 1892 a petition was addressed to the Chairman and Directors of the Great Eastern Railway asking for the reopening of the old direct Newmarket line from Great Chesterford to Six Mile Bottom. It was signed by no less a person than HRH the then Duke of York (later King George V), as well as other well-known personages interested in the Newmarket Races. Understandably, the Great Eastern Railway declined the request despite the exalted quarters from which it had emanated.

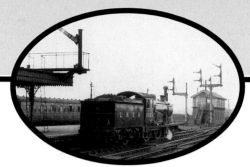

# Beyond Cambridge, and Branches

If one studies a railway map of East Anglia dated in, say, the 1950s (pre-Beeching) or — even better — in the pre-Grouping era, some thoughts arise. First, one wonders how such a predominantly agricultural area, with few large towns, could possibly have justified the capital outlay on such an extensive network. Then, one may make comparisons with our closest neighbour, France, which also had such a spider's web of railways, but financed it on different principles.

Railways in 19th century Britain appeared in an age of economic *laisser-faire* dominated by market forces, private enterprise and competition. But, as so often happens in transport, there arose a social demand for services that could not meet normal financial criteria. So, while the London–Cambridge–Ely main line fostered a number of strategic secondary routes designed to tap sources of through traffic or to forestall the entry of a competitor, it also stimulated the building of lines with little commercial justification, the so-called 'farmers' lines' usually promoted by a group of local people — landowners and businessmen as well as farmers — who felt that their community was handicapped by the lack of transport services and who were prepared to put their own money into building a rail connection. The usual hope and expectation was that, once built, it would be taken over by a main line company. Such lines had little in common with the 'strategic' lines used like chessmen by financiers such as George Hudson.

In France, the provision of an adequate rail infrastructure was regarded as something with which national or local (*Département*) organs of Government must be concerned, though operation would be entrusted to companies backed by private capital. The main lines radiating from Paris and two major cross-country routes were classed as *Chemins de fer d'Intérêt National*, but the secondary network and country branch lines was designated *Chemins de fer d'Intérêt Local,* capital for which was provided from public funds, nationally and/or locally; and in addition the concessionary railway company was guaranteed a minimum dividend, usually 5% before 1883 and 3% afterwards. The French equivalents to the British 'farmers lines' were often narrow gauge railways, a fact which reduced both capital and operating costs, but of course was a handicap in the promotion of through wagonload freight.

The nearest British counterpart to the *Chemins de fer d'Intérêt Local* was a small number of lines constructed under Light Railway Order. But nearly all the secondary network was standard gauge and had to comply with the requirements imposed by the Railway Inspectorate for passenger lines.

Looking first at the 'strategic' lines associated with the London–Cambridge axis, the outstanding one is Ely–March–Peterborough. Giving access to the Midlands and North of England, it was opened (even sooner than the obvious extension from Ely to King's Lynn) in July 1847 compared with October in that year for Lynn. In the same year came a line from Cambridge to St Ives which, with its continuation to Huntingdon, was a pawn in 'King' Hudson's game of chess against the Great Northern — a move in fact towards an ultimate link with the London and Birmingham, but one which failed. The St Ives branch only became a real route to the north when the Midland Railway built a line south from Kettering in 1866 at Huntingdon.

On the other hand, a line on the map marked only as single-track, the Ely–Newmarket line via Fordham, became part of the important 'North Country Continental' boat train route from Harwich (Parkeston Quay). Its freight also became significant and in World War 2 it carried supplies to airfields in East Anglia — leading, incidentally, to the Soham explosion described on page 127.

Lines closed today in the area under the Beeching policies include some formerly of strategic character, such as:

Cambridge–St Ives (for passengers)
Cambridge–Bedford
Ely –St Ives
March–St Ives
March–Spalding
King's Lynn–Dereham–Roudham Jct
Heacham–Wells
Bishop's Stortford–Braintree
Shelford–Sudbury

More predictably, the closed lines include many of the locally financed or 'farmers' type:

Ely station in June 1938 viewed looking north. There is as yet no sign of the intensive flow of wartime traffic to come. *R. F. Roberts*

St Margarets–Buntingford
Elsenham–Thaxted
Audley End–Saffron Walden (Bartlow)
Cambridge–Mildenhall
Denver–Stoke Ferry
King's Lynn–Hunstanton
Somersham–Ramsey

This sad catalogue excludes railways in East Anglia not associated with the Cambridge main line, such as the former Midland & Great Northern Joint. But on a more cheerful note, the following is a list of lines that remain open:

The London suburban routes* (though not here considered part of the Cambridge main line)
Broxbourne Junction–Ware and Hertford East
Stansted Junction–Stansted Airport (new line opened in 1991)

20

Cambridge–Hitchin (now with a claim to be the main line)

Cambridge–Newmarket (for Ipswich)

Ely–Snailwell Jct (for Ipswich)

Ely–Thetford (for Norwich)

Ely–March (for Peterborough)

\* excluding the closed Seven Sisters–Palace Gates and Angel Road–Lower Edmonton sections.

To trace the history of all these sections of railway, whether closed or remaining open, would require quite a substantial volume of text. But the flavour of the Cambridge line branches varies greatly; a few examples to illustrate this are:–

Broxbourne–Ware and Hertford East
St Margarets–Buntingford
Bishop's Stortford–Braintree
Elsenham–Thaxted
King's Lynn–Hunstanton.

The short branch from Broxbourne Junction to Hertford (about six miles) was promoted by the Northern & Eastern as soon as it reached Broxbourne, since the market towns of Ware and Hertford would bring in much-needed traffic receipts. Construction was easy, on level ground not far from the chalk springs at Chadwell and Amwell which fed the New River built by Sir Hugh Myddelton to give London pure drinking water. There was however a slight hitch at Ware; the railway here is between rising ground, a main road, and the waterside. A level crossing remains to this day, at a road T-junction; objections to this crossing raised by the turnpike trustees in 1843 caused some delay in the opening, which finally took place in October of that year. The branch, like the rest of the Northern & Eastern, was built to Braithwaite's 5ft gauge; but only 12 months after opening, it had to be converted to standard gauge.

It was originally single-track; when it later was doubled, the difficulties with the site at Ware obliged the retention of a single-track section through the station, which persists even today under electric traction.

*Left:* Ely station pictured in July 1955 before modernisation, which looks pretty overdue. *R. M. Casserley*

*Centre left:* Class D16 No 62530 heads north from Ely with the 2.25pm service to Peterborough on 20 May 1957. *R.C. Riley*

*Below:* Ely station photographed prior to the Grouping of 1923. *T. Middlemass*

*Right:* A truly rural scene on the important Ely–March line at Manea station in GER days. *T. Middlemass*

*Below right:* Histon station was the first station out of Cambridge on the St Ives line. *Author's Collection*

In 1858 a small independent railway, the Hertford & Welwyn Junction, was opened to link the Great Northern main line with a second station in Hertford known as Cowbridge. A single-track spur to the ECR was provided and used for freight traffic exchanges, though not for scheduled passenger train workings, except in emergency. The LNER closed the Cowbridge station to passengers in 1924 after the new Hertford North station was opened on the loop line from Wood Green via Cuffley.

The Great Eastern rebuilt Hertford East station (as it was now named) in 1888, in a rather handsome manner. It is a red-brick structure in the so-called 'free renaissance' style, with a very large and imposing *porte-cochère*. (Like the one at Audley End, it seems a trifle out of scale.) The booking hall has a decorated ceiling and there are Jacobean gables. The Great Eastern's architect, W.N. Ashbee, clearly enjoyed himself on this project!

Coming now to a branch off a branch, the Ware, Hadham & Buntingford Railway, opened in July 1863, in fact did not serve Ware owing apparently to opposition from local landowners, but instead ran from St Margarets (a station two miles east of Ware) for 13½ miles through charming Hertfordshire countryside to the market town of Buntingford. It was very much a 'farmers' line' financed by local money — not sufficiently, however, since although its Act was obtained in July 1858 acute financial shortages arose when the line was only part completed. The Eastern Counties Railway agreed to finance the completion, which did not take place until the ECR had become the GER.

The branch was single line, with originally one crossing station at Hadham. Braughing was expanded with a loop in 1892 to break up the long section from Hadham to Buntingford.

The Great Eastern maintained quite substantial station buildings at the two crossing stations, though the intermediate single-line stations at Mardock, Widford, Standon and West Mill were primitive wooden structures.

I lived for some years at Standon, commuting daily to Liverpool Street, and enjoyed the vintage GER flavour of this branch. For many years the line had served the local community and also a

St Ives station pictured in BR days with a DMU just arrived. *Author's Collection*

OAKINGTON STATION.

*Above:* Oakington station on the Cambridge–St Ives line is just visible to the left of the level crossing. *T. Middlemass*

*Below:* The King's Lynn portion of the 12.24pm service from Liverpool Street stands at the platform in Ely on 20 May 1957. *R. C. Riley*

small but growing number of daily commuters. There were in the 1930s around 11 weekday trains in each direction, taking between 28 and 35min for the journey. My morning train at 8.26am consisted of several six-wheelers with an elderly bogie corridor non-vestibuled clerestory-roofed composite carriage cascaded from main line service to this quiet backwater. Arriving in the bay platform at St Margarets, the train would be backed out on the Buntingford single line which ran alongside the Hertford track. The last coach, the composite for Liverpool Street, would be uncoupled and the train would then return to the bay. A minute or so later the train from Hertford would arrive, and after it had performed station duties it would be backed under the guidance of a shunter, to pick up the coach from Buntingford. Contact was not infrequently made with a bang that caused frowns from City gentlemen studying the *Financial Times*. Coupling effected, the complete train would set off for Broxbourne and Liverpool Street at quite a good pace, headed by an 'N7' 0-6-0T.

The return journey by the 6.00pm from Liverpool Street was notable for being performed behind an elderly J. Holden 0-6-0 goods

With Ely Cathedral in the background, Class D16 No 62530 heads away from Ely with the 2.26pm Ely-Birmingham train on 6 August 1956. *L.H. Creak.*

tender engine, which imparted a curious fore-and-aft swaying motion to the front vehicles at any speed over 40mph!

The Buntingford branch had one daily pick-up goods as well as the quite respectable passenger service mentioned. The staff were friendly; a girl once arrived at the Standon station level crossing just after the train had started. The driver saw her wave, and stopped the train on the crossing. The porter-signalman and the guard hauled the girl up into the train and it then restarted. It was sad when in June 1959 the service was reduced to a shuttle performed by a single diesel multiple-unit, and through services to Liverpool Street disappeared. There was a whispered story, perhaps apocryphal, that the shuttle DMU was diagrammed to be stabled overnight at Buntingford but the driver lived at St Margarets and found this inconvenient. The St Margarets signalman on late turn lived at Buntingford; so the two men exchanged duties, trusting that higher authority would turn a blind eye.

Quite unconnected with any trifling irregularity, the DMU service ceased in November 1964 and the branch closed completely the following year.

Northwards towards Cambridge, the next branch had some historical interest. It was based on Bishop's Stortford and it attracted local finan-

cial support, a bill for a Bishop's Stortford, Dunmow & Braintree Railway being passed by Parliament in July 1861. The Eastern Counties engineer, Robert Sinclair, was appointed engineer for the construction — foreshadowing a decision by the GER in 1863 to absorb the local company and finance the construction to completion. Brassey was the contractor and work started in April 1864. There should not have been much delay in completing a single line along the route since there were no major engineering works apart from a viaduct at Dunmow, and the total length was just under 18 miles — that is, to Braintree where an end-on junction was made with the Witham–Braintree branch that had opened in 1848.

But the cost much exceeded the estimates, and this at a time when the GER was in a poor financial condition. Wrangles with Brassey and some dissatisfaction on the part of the Board of Trade's Inspecting Officer held up the opening for public traffic until October 1869.

*Above:* Dullingham station on the Cambridge–Newmarket line. *Stations UK*

*Below:* Dullingham station viewed from track level. *T. Middlemass*

96610 Dullingham Station.

Newmarket station pictured in April 1938. *R. F. Roberts*

Although it had started as a 'farmers' line', the facts that it would link two main lines, and also that some outside interest was being shown in using part of it for a possible new railway into East Anglia, were sufficient for the Great Eastern to decide to take it over. Traffic, however, was always sparse; the original service offered only three trains each way, taking just over an hour for the 18-mile journey. By 1923 and the Grouping this had improved to six to eight trains a day (dependent on market day at the places served) and this roughly continued until closure. Journey times came down to 45–47min in LNER days, and conductor-guard working was introduced as early as 1922, involving the use of centre-gangwayed six-wheeled carriages, with open end platforms.

The first signs of danger were when Hicks Brothers of Braintree started their coach service to London in 1920, and train passengers declined. But freight revived during World War 2. Ammunition trains for the US Army Air Force used the stations at Stansted and Easton Lodge (one such train even being attacked, unsuccessfully, by a German fighter). It also was a useful diversionary route, despite its limited capacity, for occasions when the Colchester main line closed.

The first proposal to close the line was made in 1951. Closure for passengers took place in February 1952 though it remained open for freight and also special trains for the beginning and end of term at Felsted School. Final closure came in 1972.

Continuing northwards, at the summit of the Liverpool Street–Cambridge line an unusual railway formerly left the up side of Elsenham station; it was the Thaxted branch built under a Light Railway Order in 1911. It was one of the few lines that resulted from the passing of the Light Railways Act of 1896, which was based to some extent on French ideas for encouraging rural railways.

Although Thaxted is a picturesque town with a magnificent cathedral-like church, it only had about 3,000 inhabitants when some local grandees decided that its isolation from the railway should be ended. This led to the line acquiring the nickname of the 'Gin and Toffee' line after its two most important sponsors, Sir Walter Gilbey and Lee the confectionery manufacturer.

Using the procedures of the Light Railway Order meant that the Treasury contributed half the construction costs and the GER the other half. The original idea had been for a narrow gauge line, proposed in 1896, but in actual fact it was not until 1911 that the Order was secured and then for a standard gauge branch. The total cost was £31,250 and landowners gave the land free. The 5½-mile route was opened in April 1913, with five down and four up trains daily.

Light Railways were (and are) restricted to a maximum speed of 25mph and this gave a jour-

*Above:* A view of Hertford East station which illustrates the grand *porte-cochère* — a facility that was a trifle out of scale. *Author*

*Below:* Ware station — a view which shows the single platform and constricted site.
*T. Middlemass*

*Ware Station, G. E. R.*

*Above:* An up train from Hertford East enters St Margarets station on 16 April 1957.
*R. M. Casserley*

*Below:* A train bound for Buntingford is seen leaving St Margarets.
*British Rail*

Buntingford station exterior; this was much the most substantial building on the branch.
*T. Middlemass*

ney time of 22–28min; there was one intermediate station and two halts. The Thaxted station was inconveniently far from the town; it had one short platform.

Conductor-guard operation was in force to minimise staff costs. As on the Braintree branch, old GER compartment six-wheelers were converted to open-ends. But when a coach service to London started, this, together with the growth in car ownership enabling people to get to Elsenham station in half the time of the branch train, spelt the end. Closure came in September 1952, an Eastern National bus service replacing the trains.

The next line to be described, although now closed, had, in common with the still-open Hertford line, good financial justification for its construction. The Lynn & Hunstanton Railway opened in October 1862 and was, as Professor Jack Simmons and Stanley C. Jenkins have related, a particularly interesting example of a partnership between a local landowner, in this case Henry L'Estrange, and railway promotion intended to create a new seaside resort.

Buntingford station's only platform; its simplicity contrasts with the relatively substantial station building seen from the road. *T. Middlemass*

King's Lynn viewed in steam days. *Author's Collection*

L'Estrange acted as a developer, giving free of charge much of the land required for the construction of the railway, which in consequence was built for no more than about £4,000 a mile. Unlike some later failed seaside developments based on a new railway (such as that at All-Hallows-on-Sea in Kent) Hunstanton and its railway prospered together. The Great Eastern worked it for 50% of the receipts and the original capital earned dividends around 10%. It was perhaps a pity that over-optimism led to an extension being built from Heacham to Wells and separately capitalised as the West Norfolk Railway: its profitability never matched that of the original Lynn & Hunstanton, a fact reflected in the terms under which the combined undertaking was absorbed by the Great Eastern in 1887, a year after the dividend on the original capital had been 11¾%. The Great Eastern therefore had good reason traditionally to regard Hunstanton as a valued end of the Cambridge main line, something reflected in the quality of train services to and from London for many years.

Apart from profitability, the Lynn & Hunstanton Railway gained what may be termed 'snob' value from the very first year of its opening when the Sandringham estate was bought for the use of the then Prince of Wales. The frequency of Royal specials gave the line added importance and Wolferton station (only 2½ miles from Sandringham House) originally a fairly simple structure, was rebuilt in 1898 with ornate Tudor-style buildings on each platform. The main Royal waiting rooms, panelled in oak, were on the down platform.

The Great Eastern showed its sense of the importance of Hunstanton by building a substantial resort hotel called The Sandringham; it complemented the railway's Felix hotel at Felixstowe on the Colchester main line, also something of a 'mushroom' resort fostered by the GER.

Through trains from Liverpool Street to Hunstanton became a feature in the Edwardian period with portions working to and from St Pancras, the Liverpool Street services including some with restaurant cars for the full journey. In 1939 the LNER continued this practice with the 11.55am and 5.49pm down, and 7.12am and 4.50pm up expresses. The 'Eastern Belle' Pullman excursion train was also a visitor to Hunstanton, now and again. That feature was not reinstated by British Railways after Nationalisation but the resort briefly gained a named train, the 'Fenman', which included a buffet car.

Dieselisation on the Eastern Region meant that Hunstanton was treated as a branch station, main line trains terminating at King's Lynn and passengers having to change there into a DMU. The effect was to drive people to prefer the use of their cars; the usual vicious spiral of service cuts leading to declining patronage producing yet more service cuts followed, and the Hunstanton line finally closed in May 1969. Wolferton station was sold and became a private dwelling, with the Royal Waiting Room restored and turned into a museum open to the public.

33

*Above:* King's Lynn motive power depot seen on 15 April 1947, showing a variety of locomotives 'on shed'. *H. C. Casserley*

*Below:* An immaculate 'Claud' stands outside the depot at King's Lynn in LNER livery.
*H. C. Casserley*

A line that, like the Dunmow and Braintree route, linked the Cambridge and Colchester main lines, is that from Shelford, just south of Cambridge, to Haverhill, Sudbury and Mark's Tey (for Colchester). It can more properly be regarded as an adjunct to the Colchester main line since its most important part was the still-open section from Mark's Tey to Sudbury.

In 1939 this typical ex-GER cross-country trip for the 50 miles from Colchester to Cambridge took about 2¼hr with 15 intermediate stops; there were five trains daily each way. Closure, except for the Mark's Tey–Sudbury section must have been seen as inevitable with the dawn of the motor age.

Saffron Walden is an historic town and market centre like Thaxted. As at Thaxted, local people of importance (in this case the Gibson family of bankers) sponsored the rail connection by putting up their own money.

The ceremony of cutting the first sod was rather spoiled by the fact that no one had remembered to provide a spade for the occasion! Despite this, the Saffron Walden Railway opened from Audley End in November 1865 and until the arrival of the motor age was probably justified,

with quite a reasonable connecting service over the 1¾ miles from Audley End to Saffron Walden where several local industries were based. The extension to Bartlow, 5½ miles on, was however a costly mistake, based on the hope of running through trains over the Cambridge–Colchester route (despite the junction at Bartlow facing the wrong way, towards Cambridge). It led to a financial crisis, solved by the GER taking over the Saffron Walden Railway in 1877. But, although DMUs took over the service for a short time, the traffic was insignificant and the line closed completely in December 1964.

These rather different examples illustrate what has happened in the area served by the Cambridge line where the Ordnance Survey maps show with such depressing frequency the legend 'Cse of dismantled rly' — not much of an epitaph on so much local initiative and railway enterprise.

Ivatt Class C12 4-4-2T No 67374 and a stopping train are pictured at King's Lynn on 2 September 1955. *H. C. Casserley*

*Above left:* A stopping train leaves King's Lynn on 15 April 1947 behind a J. Holden Class F3 tank No 7149. *H. C. Casserley*

*Above:* The scene at King's Lynn on 15 April 1947 sees No 7149 awaiting the signal. *H. C. Casserley*

*Left:* Shunting is in progress at King's Lynn on 21 May 1957, with No 62592 acting as station pilot. *R. C. Riley*

*Above:* A view on the Hunstanton line near King's Lynn in June 1938; the photographer is looking towards Hunstanton. *R. F. Roberts*

*Below:* One of the LNER Pullman sets was used on Sundays for a number of day trips to resorts, including, on occasions, Hunstanton. These were known as the 'Eastern Belle' trips. This particular trip is being hauled by Gresley Class B17/2 No 2811. *British Rail*

*Top:* Hunstanton station is seen on 19 June 1938. The photographer is looking towards the buffer-stops. *R. F. Roberts*

*Above:* A Colchester-bound cross-country train is about to leave Cambridge in May 1956 behind Class E4 2-4-0 No 62792. *R. M. Casserley*

*Above:* A stopping train from Haverhill passes
Trumpington on 24 September 1949 headed by an 'E4'
2-4-0 of J. Holden design. *D. A. Dant/The Gresley Society*

*Below:* Linton station on the Cambridge–Colchester
line pictured prior to the Grouping.
*T. Middlemass*

*Top:* A Mildenhall branch train is pictured near Ditton halt on 19 April 1952 with 'E4' No 62783 in charge. *D. A. Dant/The Gresley Society*

*Above:* A Cambridge–Bletchley train, caught near Sandy, is about to cross over the Great Northern main line. The loco, still bearing the short-lived 'British Railways' in full on its tender, is a Gresley rebuild (with round-topped firebox) of a classic GER 4-4-0 No 62535. *C. W. Goslin/The Gresley Society*

*Right:* Saffron Walden station on 9 December 1910; this was one of the two intermediate stations on the Audley End–Bartlow line.
*National Railway Museum/ Crown Copyright Reserved*

*Below:* Ivatt Class C12 No 67375, the branch line locomotive, takes water at Saffron Walden on 3 March 1951. *L. R. Peters/ The Gresley Society*

*Above:* Potton LNWR station, on the Cambridge–Bletchley line, viewed in about 1900. *T. Middlemass*

*Below:* Pictured at the end of the Thaxted branch is the shuttle from Elsenham on 3 March 1951 with motive power provided by Class J69 0-6-0T No 68609 — note the tramcar-like carriages. *L. R. Peters/ The Gresley Society*

# War and Peace with the Great Northern

Relations between the Great Northern and the Eastern Counties (from 1862 the Great Eastern) varied over the years between open hostility, suspicious horse-trading, and finally full collaboration — ending of course in 1923 with the Grouping which brought both railways into the Southern Area of the London & North Eastern Railway. The frontier points associated with the Cambridge main line where conflicts of interests arose were limited to a few — Hertford, Shepreth (between Cambridge and Royston), St Ives, March and Peterborough. At all of these a *modus vivendi* had eventually to be worked out between the GNR and the GER.

In the early days, the Great Northern could feel happy at having fought off the threat of an Eastern Counties trunk line to Yorkshire, but it soon turned its attention to Cambridge. Edmund Denison, the pugnacious GNR Chairman, told his shareholders in 1851 in his own inimitable way of his determination to get there. 'If there be any Eastern Counties shareholders here I will tell them,' he said, 'with perfect respect that my duty will be to go to Cambridge. I will do it in the most amicable and harmonious way possible, if they will permit me, but go I must and undoubtedly I shall.'

The Great Northern had not yet opened King's Cross station when Denison spoke but it had already leased a line pointing at Cambridge, the Royston & Hitchin Railway, under powers obtained in 1847. This little company had started as a component of an Oxford–Cambridge cross-country link, officially supported by the two universities. A bill based on plans prepared by Joseph Locke was introduced into Parliament in 1846; it proposed a single-track route passing through Thame, Aylesbury, Dunstable, Luton, Hitchin and Royston. Parliament however seems

to have had doubts about the sincerity of the desire of the two ancient universities for closer contacts and only approved a railway 13 miles long, double-tracked, from Hitchin to Royston. The Great Northern decided to take a lease of this short line and to persevere with attempts to get it extended to Cambridge.

Meanwhile the Eastern Counties had been promoting a line of their own from Cambridge to Bedford, passing through Shepreth, about halfway between Cambridge and Royston. This line to Bedford was actually authorised but construction was delayed by the weak financial position of the ECR.

The Royston & Hitchin company then obtained powers to extend as far as a junction with the intended ECR station at Shepreth, and the full Hitchin–Shepreth line was opened for traffic in August 1851. Undaunted by the continuing absence of a Shepreth–Cambridge rail link, the GNR arranged for its trains terminating at Shepreth to connect there with a four-horse omnibus service to Trinity Street in Cambridge. Passengers from London had to change trains at Hitchin as well as from train to bus at Shepreth. Even so, the best through service took only 15 min longer than the best ECR trains from Bishopsgate. The GNR also tried to attract traffic by cutting fares, compared with the ECR, by one shilling (5p) first class and sixpence (2½p) second class.

However, this burst of enterprise was to be short-lived, because in 1851 the GNR and the ECR negotiated a 'treaty' covering their competitive traffics. The ECR, under its terms, took over the lease of the Royston & Hitchin and, finally abandoning the idea of going to Bedford, built a single line south from Cambridge to Shepreth, opening in April 1852.

Needless to say, the ECR did not facilitate

through services from King's Cross to Cambridge, but merely ran local trains. But the treaty was only in force for 14 years, and after it ended in 1866 the GNR regained possession of the line from Hitchin as far as the end-on junction at Shepreth; and by now it also enjoyed running powers to Cambridge which Parliament had granted two years earlier. Thereafter there were always to be through London–Cambridge train services from King's Cross.

Apart from Cambridge, the most important differences with the Great Northern were over actual or potential traffic exchanges and through running at St Ives, March, Peterborough,

access to the South Yorkshire coalfield centred upon Doncaster. Nearly 20 years of Parliamentary battles and behind-the-scenes negotiations had to take place before the Great Eastern was to secure its objective; at times other companies with interests in the area — the Lancashire & Yorkshire, and the North Eastern — were involved. The details of this epic struggle are given by C.H. Grinling in his *History of the Great Northern Railway* and C.J. Allen in *The Great Eastern Railway*. Eventually in 1879 agreement was reached for the creation of a 'Great Northern & Eastern Railways Committee' to own and manage a route from March to Doncaster, partly fol-

Wisbech and King's Lynn. The history of the Great Northern's attempts to penetrate into Norfolk, and the ECR/GER attempts to get 'mileage' out of traffic to and from the north, is a long and complicated one. However, the general treaty on charges and facilities in force from 1852 to 1866 covered not merely the GNR's access to Cambridge but the working of all the 'frontier points' with joint ownership of sections of line such as St Ives–March and St Ives— Huntingdon.

But by the early 1860s the GER, looking to the end of the treaty period, revived its old ambition of becoming a great trunk line to the north. It engaged in a long battle to reach Yorkshire by means of an entirely new line from March. Although York was an ultimate objective, the principal source of revenue would be from

lowing existing lines but between Spalding and Lincoln using a new direct railway built by the GNR over which the GER had running powers. It was opened in August 1882.

The first gain to the Cambridge main line was the additional coal traffic, much of it destined either for London or Thamesside docks; there followed through passenger trains from Liverpool Street to Doncaster and later York. But it was the intermediate towns that really benefited from this ultimate projection of Cambridge's main line services over what the Great Eastern's publicity department later called the 'Cathedrals Route' because it linked Ely, Lincoln and York.

The 'Joint Line', as the route from March to Doncaster was always known to generations of railwaymen, had the advantage for heavy freight trains of being almost entirely free from gradients of any significance, at any rate north of Cambridge. In the 1950s when coal traffic to London was still important, serious consideration was given by the Eastern Region of British Railways to the economics of electrifying the Joint Line, which could be done, it was thought, at a comparatively low cost per route-mile. There were few overbridges to be raised to accommodate the 25kV overhead catenary, and little multiple track. Unfortunately the decline in freight traffic, already clear by 1960, eliminated the financial case. Today, sadly, the March–Spalding section has been closed and the access to the 'Joint Line' is via Peterborough.

*Below left:* Hitchin station, from which the attack on Cambridge was launched, viewed in GNR days. *Author's Collection*

*Below:* The down platform of Hitchin station seen around the turn of the century. *Author's Collection*

*Bottom:* The exterior of Hitchin station, GNR, with apparently a dog-cart and a bicycle-type of 'machine' awaiting a train. *Author's Collection*

*Above left:* Baldock station, GNR. *T. Middlemass*

*Above:* Shepreth station — passenger information was evidently a high priority for the staff! *Stations UK*

*Left:* Meldreth station pictured under GNR ownership showing a surprisingly busy goods yard for such a small place. Note the wagon turntable on the extreme left. *Author's Collection*

*Left:* Shepreth station viewed in GNR days. This illustration shows clearly the sharp curve that enforces a severe speed restriction even today.
*Author's Collection*

*Above:* Letchworth old station showing a crowd (surely not commuters?) waiting to board a GNR train. *T. Middlemass*

*Left:* The new station at Letchworth, which was built to serve the Garden City. *T. Middlemass*

# The Saga of Cambridge Station

When the railway reached Cambridge in 1845 the town, despite its strategic location and its academic importance, had only about 25,000 inhabitants and the university numbered well under 2,000 undergraduates. It was however a growing business centre with industries that included brewing, malting, milling, brickmaking and printing.

The cautious welcome that the university gave the railway seems to have been assured only by a stipulation that the station should be sited not less than one mile from Great St Mary's Church in the town centre. Furthermore, in order to preserve the morals of undergraduates from the dangers presented by easy access to the delights of London, the university authorities followed an example set by Oxford, and ensured that Section 184 of the Eastern Counties Railway Act of 1844 contained a proviso that university officers defined as 'Proctors with or without their servants (i.e. the "Bulldogs") and the Heads and Tutors of Colleges and Halls and the Marshal and Yeoman Bedell of the University' were to have free access to all parts of the station around the times of arrival and departure of trains. The object of this was to secure enforcement of a provision that 'any person who shall be a member of the University *or suspected of being such,* (my italics) not having the degree of Master of Arts or Bachelor of Civil Law or Medicine', may be prevented from travelling for 24hr, notwithstanding that he may have paid his fare. (As a small consolation, the railway would be exempt from civil actions for damages from people wrongly prevented from travelling, provided any fare paid had been refunded to them.)

In addition, the university secured a prohibition of Sunday trains between the hours of 10am and 5pm, 'no passenger to be taken up or set down at the Cambridge station or within three miles of the same under a penalty of £5 for each offence'.

Despite these restrictions (soon quietly ignored but not finally repealed until 1908) — and perhaps partly because the Great Western Railway had not treated Oxford very well in the matter of a station — the ECR's architect Sancton Wood was commissioned to design quite an impressive building which survives in essentials today. It comprises a long classical block in local brick with stone dressings, its main feature being the extended *porte-cochère* or colonnade which covered arrival and departure roadways for cabs and private carriages. On the first floor were rooms for railway offices, which continued in use throughout many organisational changes.

The feature which has always caused most interest is that Cambridge is a 'single-sided' station. One long platform serves both up and down trains, though there are bays at each end accommodating trains that start or finish at Cambridge. Single-sided stations were fairly common in the early days; Brunel built them at Reading, Slough, Taunton, Exeter and Gloucester. (Apart from Gloucester, however, his stations comprised two quite separate up and down platforms, end-to-end but not joined together.)

Curiously enough, a single-sided station on a double-line railway survives just a few miles from the Cambridge main line, at Ware, though the design here was not dictated by choice but by the severe limitations of the site.

As long as traffic remained fairly light, so that the arrival of up and down trains was not likely to coincide, this arrangement had its advantages. Passengers were relieved of the necessity to cross footbridges or subways. The centralisation

of facilities was economical, particularly in staff requirements. But the original platform was short and inadequate, and soon had to be supplemented.

The history of the separate up platform is complicated. Canon R.B. Fellows, who wrote about the railways of Cambridge, states that 'soon after the station was opened' a wooden island platform was built for up trains. This appears to have been constructed in 1848 and to have been only a temporary affair, replaced by another in 1850. This second up platform was linked to the main platform by means of a narrow footbridge and a subway for luggage trolleys, liable to flooding.

Both up and down trains used the island for a time, the original platform having apparently been relegated, mainly if not completely, to the parcels traffic. But the inconvenience of having to use a narrow footbridge caused many complaints and in 1856 the original platform was restored to use by down trains. Then in 1863, this platform was lengthened sufficiently to accommodate both up and down trains via crossovers in the middle, and the island platform was demolished.

The idea of an island platform for up trains was revived in 1899 when the GER proposed a comprehensive rebuilding, but there was strong opposition in the town to having to use a footbridge and the proposal was dropped. The single

Cambridge station in GER days seen with canopy (long since removed) and array of waiting vehicles including a hansom cab, the 'Bull Hotel' horse bus, and an early motor bus. *Cambridgeshire Collection, Cambridgeshire Libraries*

platform was lengthened, and bays added at the north and south ends, in the course of time. In 1908 its length was increased to 1,515ft, later still to 1,650ft, and the tracks nearest the platform slewed to the east, to permit widening of the platform by 11ft. A new awning was also built which partly relieved the constriction caused by the previous awning's supporting columns on a narrow platform.

Sancton Wood's building block, which included railway District Offices above the station's passenger facilities, was internally remodelled in 1863 and again in 1908. A major 19th century change was the extension of the booking hall to enclose the central section of the colonnade. More recently British Rail has replaced the old booking office with a large travel centre.

Externally, a marked improvement has come from the cleaning of the brickwork and the picking out in colour of the armorial bearings which Sancton Wood included in the spandrels of the columns. These originally combined the arms of a selection of the colleges with those of the town and certain local dignitaries — a rather arbitrary selection. These have now been revised to be

52

*Above:* An LNWR train for Bletchley is about to leave Cambridge, *c*1900, behind a 2-4-2T. *T. Middlemass*

*Right:* Cambridge Station platform, *c*1900, showing the bracket signals controlling the famous scissors crossover in the centre of the station. *Author's Collection*

*Below:* Cambridge station platform; the pillars supporting the awning were removed in the 1908 reconstruction. *Author's Collection*

more comprehensive so far as the colleges are concerned.

While originating and terminating trains largely used bays at the end of the long main platform, use of the latter for both down and up through trains involved providing a scissors crossover in the central area which remains in use today, the tradition being formerly that down trains used the northern half of the long platform and up trains the southern half.

For many years, outside the platform tracks, there were through goods lines and, beyond them, stabling sidings. The layout has, however, been somewhat simplified since electrification.

The main locomotive depot of the Great Eastern was at the north end in steam days. The south end saw both a shed for the Great Northern locomotives (closed in 1931) and one for the London & North Western engines working to Bletchley. The main motive power depot north of the station used to produce a smoky

*Above left:* Class J15 0-6-0 No 65460 waits at the south end of Platform 1 at Cambridge station; in the adjacent bay a DMU shows that the days of steam in the area are numbered. *P. Rutherford*

*Below left:* The view looking north from Cambridge in 1913. *L. D. Peters/The Gresley Society*

*Below:* Cambridge South signalbox pictured in 1927. *The Railway Engineer*

and acrid atmosphere which hung over this whole quarter of the city and darkened the buildings.

The progressive lengthening of the main platform has been accompanied by other changes. There were formerly four signal-boxes: North, Central, South and Hills Road Junction (controlling the Bletchley line connections). These have been reduced, first by amalgamating South and Hills Road boxes, then eliminating the Central box which controlled the scissors crossover, and today a single powerbox controls not just the station but the surrounding rail network.

Cambridge long had two signalling features not known elsewhere on the system. One was the lower-quadrant powered semaphores that controlled arrivals and departures and the central scissors crossover. The other was the use, as ground signals controlling shunting movements, of miniature semaphores made of toughened rubber. The reason for this unusual material was that the signals were somewhat tight to gauge, and consequently needed to be protected against damage should they be touched by a moving vehicle.

The very sharp curve to the Newmarket line, which traversed the station sidings, was replaced by a new and easier curve at Coldham Lane, half a mile to the north, in 1896.

Cambridge station, being just under one mile from the Market Square which may be considered the city centre, produced a profitable business for, originally, horse cabs, and, later, taxis. In 1880 a horse tramway was laid along Station

Road to the centre and this operated, with some vicissitudes, until 1914 when bus competition finally forced the withdrawal of the trams; the last stretch of tramway rails lasted until 1927. The buses were originally operated by the Ortona Bus Company (later absorbed by Eastern Counties a subsidiary of the Tilling Group).

Would Cambridge have done better with a station more conveniently close to the centre? The Eastern Counties and Great Eastern never contemplated such a removal, but the Royston & Hitchin company's bill of 1848 provided for a new Cambridge terminus close to the Botanic Garden; this site was also proposed in the unsuccessful Cambridge & Shepreth Junction Railway bill of 1850. The following year the GNR's bill for the Shepreth–Cambridge link proposed a terminus adjacent to Silver Street, in St Botolph's. This would have passed 'under the windows of Peterhouse' and the University Members of Parliament (the Senior and Junior Burgesses) successfully opposed it.

There is a legend that when the Prince of Wales, the future King Edward VII, was an undergraduate at Trinity College, his mother, Queen Victoria, expressed satisfaction that the railway station was not too easy of access, fearing that her son otherwise would be tempted to jump on a train for London whenever he felt inclined to visit the West End.

However that may be, generations of Cambridge residents, dons and undergraduates have cursed the lengthy stretches of St Andrew's Street, Regent Street, Hills Road and Station Road when time has been short for them to catch their trains and the station clock has come into view with its threatening message.

Cambridge as an operating and commercial district was interesting to a career railwayman since it offered something of almost every type of traffic — main line expresses, through heavy freights, branch line locals, cross-country workings, and Royal specials. Several senior managers in the London & North Eastern and later, in British Railways 'cut their teeth' there.

Cambridge also acquired a Railway Club founded in 1911–12 as a branch of the London-based Railway Club. It fell upon poor times until it was reconstituted in 1935 as a university society. The club was fortunate in attracting the interest of Sir Nigel Gresley, who presented a trophy to be awarded annually to the winner of a speaking competition. The club has a modern counterpart in the Cambridge Railway Circle.

The LMS three-car diesel multiple-unit used for a time on through services between Oxford and Cambridge via Bletchley during the 1930s. *National Railway Museum/Crown Copyright Reserved*

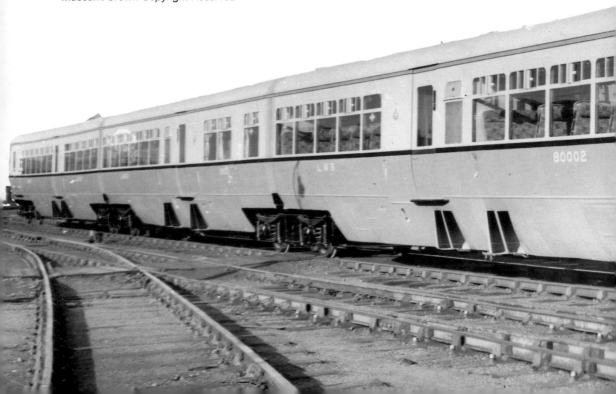

Gresley's unique water-tube high-pressure boilered 4-6-4, No 10000, at Cambridge North on 22 May 1933 returns to Doncaster after being on exhibition at Southend-on-Sea.
*A. Garraway/The Gresley Society*

*Above:* A King's Cross-bound express leaves Cambridge behind two small Atlantics some time in the 1930s. *National Railway Museum/Crown Copyright Reserved*

*Below:* An unusual working: Gresley's unique No 10000 heads the 2.6pm Sunday train, from Cambridge to King's Cross, in November 1937. *R. F. Roberts*

*Above:* The Mildenhall branch train enters Cambridge, hauled by an elderly 0-6-0, LNER No 7548, in January 1938. *R. F. Roberts*

*Below:* An immaculate 'Claud Hamilton', No 8783, draws away from Cambridge on 16 April 1938. *E. R. Wethersett/Ian Allan Library*

*Top:* Ex-LMS '4F' 0-6-0 No 44273 heads for St. Ives from Chesterton Junction Cambridge with the 1.15pm Tennyson Field — Whitemoor coal empties on 5 June 1961. *G D King*

*Above:* An exhibition of locomotives and rolling stock was held at Cambridge in May 1938. Amongst exhibits was 'Claud Hamilton' No 8783 and 'B17' No 2818. *A. Garraway/The Gresley Society*

*Top:* The Royal Train, *en route* from Wolferton (for Sandringham) to King's Cross, passes Cambridge in January 1938. The loco is 'Claud Hamilton' class 4-4-0 No 8783, one of the pair of 'Royal' engines.
*R. F. Roberts*

*Above:* On 22 May 1959 'B2' 4-6-0 No 61607 *Blickling* starts the 10.40am Cambridge — Liverpool Street stopping service out of Great Chesterford. *C. J. Sarah*

*Left:* Engines stand at the water cranes outside the shed on 16 April 1945. Wartime grime is still in evidence. *H. C. Casserley*

*Left:* 'Coaling up' at Cambridge on 6 April 1946 as 0-6-0 No 8279 receives attention. *H. C. Casserley*

*Bottom:* A Wisbech & Upwell 'tramway' locomotive, No 7136, pictured on a visit to Cambridge on 6 April 1946. *H. C. Casserley*

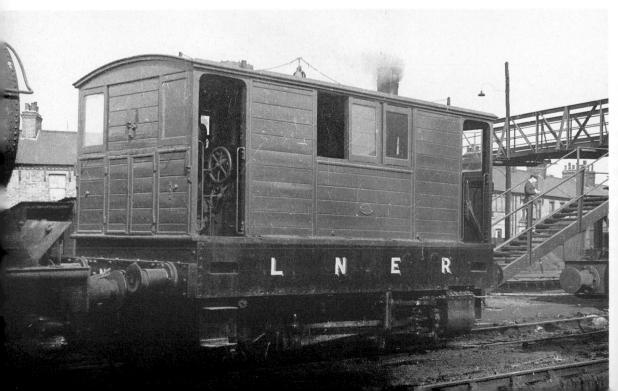

*Above:* A 'B12/3', No 1565, in full green livery after wartime austerity, stands outside Cambridge blowing off hard, on a day in 1947. *L. R. Peters/The Gresley*

*Below:* A 'B17' ('Sandringham') class 4-6-0 *Melton Hall* stands outside Cambridge on 7 April 1946. *H. C. Casserley*

*Above:* These power signals, pictured in April 1947, controlled the scissors crossing until replaced by colour-lights under modernisation. *H. C. Casserley*

*Left:* The London end of the long platform seen in April 1947. This photograph shows how the awning supports restricted movement of barrows. *H. C. Casserley*

*Below left:* A Liverpool Street-bound train is ready to depart from Cambridge on 15 April 1947 behind Class B17 No 1628 *Harewood House. H. C. Casserley*

*Above right:* No 62582 is seen again, this time on shed at Cambridge, after having worked the up 'Fenman' from King's Lynn on 20 May 1957. *R. C. Riley*

*Right:* The 10.15am service to King's Lynn via March leaves northbound with 'Super-Claud' No 62582 at the head on 20 May 1957. *R. C. Riley*

*Above left:* BR Standard 'Britannia' class No 70001 *Lord Hurcomb* takes water at Cambridge whilst working a down Norwich express in 1959. *L. R. Peters/The Gresley Society*

*Below left:* The frontage of Cambridge station pictured in the 1980s, showing the enclosure of the colonnade. *Author*

*Above:* Work in progress on the enclosure of the colonnade. *Cambridgeshire Libraries, Cambridgeshire Collection*

*Below:* The station's famous scissors crossover after electrification. *Author*

*Above:* A view looking north along the platform at Cambridge station, 1992. *Author*

*Below:* A 'Sprinter' bound for Stansted Airport arrives at Cambridge from Birmingham in 1992. *Author*

# Nineteenth Century Trains and Locomotives

In the 19th century, as indeed in the 20th, the Cambridge line was bedevilled by several factors — the character of the area served, the engineering of the route, and the uncertainties of managerial policy. Commercially, towns such as Bishop's Stortford, Cambridge, Ely and King's Lynn could not compare with the industrial centres of the North and Midlands, nor with Bristol, Exeter or Cardiff. They were not so distant from London, or so far apart, that substantial rates and fares could be charged on a mileage basis; long non-stop runs were not commercially justified.

The engineering of the route was initially hampered by the weak finances of the Eastern Counties as well as of the Northern & Eastern. Where the ground was undulating, heavy earthworks were avoided as far as possible, and this led to curves and quite severe, if short, gradients. Moreover, in order to keep down expenditure, a rather restrictive loading gauge was adopted. In later times this could cause problems when 'foreign' vehicles — particularly those from companies with a more generous loading gauge such as the Great Western — worked on to the ECR/GER system. (This was incidentally the reason for the unique ground signals or 'dods' later installed at Cambridge, referred to in Chapter 6.)

Another adverse factor was the track geometry. Much, if not most, of the ECR was laid out lacking transition curves. The maximum permissible speed of trains was limited at various places by the abrupt change from straight track to a curve of constant radius, which also gave uncomfortable riding. In modern times, there has had to be a good deal of realignment to insert proper transition curves, making the change from straight to curve progressive by gradually reducing the radius.

Management policy seems to have varied, so far as express train services are concerned, between bursts of enterprise separated by periods of lethargy. Traditionally, the most ambitious performance was to run non-stop between London and Cambridge — something that kept appearing and then disappearing from the timetable. After the early example of enterprise with the Norwich service mentioned in Chapter 2 (with a 19-mile dash at 43.8mph from Shoreditch to Broxbourne), the ECR settled down to a jog-trot performance in which the claims of intermediate stations, such as Tottenham, Broxbourne and Bishop's Stortford prevailed over any feeling that Cambridge deserved better things.

There is however evidence that the value of Cambridge as a tourist centre, and its potential for excursionists, was early recognised by the ECR, since in 1851 the then Vice-Chancellor (Dr G.E. Corrie, Master of Jesus College) sent the board his celebrated letter protesting about the railway's 'decision to carry foreigners and other unseemly persons... who having no regard for Sunday themselves, would inflict their presence in the University on that day of rest... the contemplated arrangements are as distasteful to the University authorities as they must be to Almighty God...'

It is not clear whether the ECR directors had deliberately decided to break the restriction upon Sunday trains contained in their Act of 1844, or whether they had forgotten it.

The Great Eastern entered upon one of its major periods of enterprise in the 1870s. Even before then, in 1868, it had become possible to run Cambridge line trains into and out of St Pancras which, if rather optimistically described as a 'West End' terminus, was certainly nearer to Mayfair than Bishopsgate. Then came in 1876 the almost simultaneous openings of Liverpool

Shelford Station. 5821

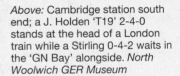

STANSTED. G.E.R.

*Above:* Cambridge station south end; a J. Holden 'T19' 2-4-0 stands at the head of a London train while a Stirling 0-4-2 waits in the 'GN Bay' alongside. *North Woolwich GER Museum*

*Left:* Shelford station and level crossing pictured at the end of the 19th century. *T. Middlemass*

*Below left:* Stansted station seen with a down Cambridge express approaching in GER days. *T. Middlemass*

Street and the Clapton to Copper Mill 'cut-off', the latter reducing distances by 2½ miles compared with via Stratford.

The GER also acquired in 1874 a new chairman, C.H. Parkes, who took a keen interest in train timetabling and who was nicknamed 'Punctuality Parkes' from his constant harping upon the importance of actually doing what the timetable offered. In 1883 E. Foxwell, a severe critic of railway performance, wrote that the Great Eastern 'when unharassed by floods, is a most punctual line'. He also commented that the GER was 'a line which has lately undergone a pleasant metamorphosis from a state of ludicrous inefficiency into that of a well-equipped and promising express line'.

The completion of the Joint Line in 1882 described in Chapter 5 was followed by a progressive extension of passenger services out of Liverpool Street, to Doncaster from September 1882 and eventually (by agreement with the North Eastern Railway) into York in November 1892. As however Liverpool Street to York was 214¾ miles compared with 188 miles from King's Cross to York, through passenger travel could hardly by expected. In any case, the primary purpose in building the Joint Line had been freight, and the passenger timetable seemed to reflect this. Timings between Ely, March, Spalding, Sleaford, Lincoln and Doncaster were always leisurely, though occasionally an enterprising driver would take advantage of the flat terrain to run fast and regain lost time. E.L. Ahrons, in his inimitable way, recorded a journey on the best train of the day in the 1880s , the 4.48pm from Doncaster, behind a Massey Bromley 7ft 6in single, when time was regained to March with one or two spurts at 70mph. But at March, he recounted, one of the Worsdell 2-4-0s backed on, 'after which we strolled gingerly across the fens in the direction of Ely and Cambridge... it reminded me of the American train on which the immortal Mark Twain proposed that the cow-catcher should be transferred from the front to the rear, because there was no possible chance of overtaking the cow, but, on the other hand, there was no safeguard to prevent the cow from strolling into the train and biting the passengers'.

Ahrons found that things were better on the Ely and Norwich lines. In 1885 there were nonstops between London and Cambridge on one of which he recorded a time of 72min giving quite a creditable average speed of 46.4mph.

A particular feature of the Cambridge line was its connection to Newmarket, and Cambridge station had for long the distinction of handling more horse boxes than any other station in Britain. Perhaps after all, the closure of the direct Newmarket Railway in 1858 had been a mistake! On one day in 1874 six special trains were run to Newmarket from Bishopsgate, two having portions from St Pancras which were joined on at Tottenham.

Royal specials to and from Wolferton, for Sandringham, were to be a feature of the Cambridge main line for almost a century. But the first 'Royal' anticipated the opening of the Hunstanton line by some 15 years. The Prince Consort was to be installed as Chancellor of Cambridge University on 5 July 1847 and he and Queen Victoria used the Eastern Counties to make a journey from Tottenham to Cambridge. Presumably, despite the length of the road journey from Buckingham Palace to Tottenham, the use of Bishopsgate was avoided to escape the ceremonial involved whenever the Sovereign enters the City of London.

The ECR had to borrow a Royal saloon for this trip as it had none of its own. The train left Tottenham at 11.20, with a stop for locomotive purposes at Bishop's Stortford, and arrived at Cambridge at 1.08pm: the return on a later day was, like the outward trip, accompanied by George Hudson, then Chairman of the ECR.

Sandringham was used in March 1863 for the honeymoon of the Prince of Wales, later King Edward VII, and the future Queen Alexandra; the locomotive that worked the Royal train was specially painted cream and garlanded. Thirty years later another Royal honeymoon special was provided for the then Duke and Duchess of York (later King George V and Queen Mary). This train was notable by being drawn by an oil-fired locomotive, 2-4-0 No 761.

The Tottenham & Hampstead Junction Railway was opened in July 1868. After the connection with the Midland main line at the western end was effected in 1870 it became possible to run the Royal specials into and out of St Pancras to avoid entering the City of London. The Great Eastern fell in with the wishes of Buckingham Palace in this regard, although it involved the payment of tolls to the T&H, and to the Midland for the use of St Pancras. Royal specials, like all other trains, had to reverse at King's Lynn to reach Wolferton, only 6½ miles away. King's Lynn engines and crews worked to and from Wolferton; Cambridge engines and men between Lynn and London.

Cambridge station pictured with an up train headed by an early Ivatt 4-4-0. *Author's Collection*

In 1896 Acworth could write in *The Railways of England* about the complexity of the Great Eastern's working at Ely where 'there arrive, within an interval of about twenty minutes, in addition to these two trains from the East from Lowestoft and Yarmouth, trains from London, from Lynn and Hunstanton, from Doncaster, from Ipswich, Bury St Edmunds and Newmarket, and from Peterborough. In the course of a short half-hour, everything gets itself re-sorted somehow... two trains are careering away (for Liverpool Street and St Pancras respectively), a third to Doncaster, a fourth to Peterborough, a fifth to Lynn, a sixth to Newmarket *en route* to Ipswich and Colchester, and a seventh, which has never entered Ely Station at all, to Norwich on its way to Yarmouth and Lowestoft.'

The 19th century saw plenty of changes in the Great Northern's London–Cambridge train services. First, in 1851 (from the temporary terminus at Maiden Lane, before King's Cross opened) there was the curious rail and horse-omnibus service mentioned in Chapter 5, which ended with the 1851–1865 'treaty' after which it became possible if inadvisable to use GNR trains with changes at both Hitchin and Shepreth. The journey took almost 3hr.

Once the GNR got its running powers into Cambridge and built its own engine shed there, real competition began. There was a separate passenger booking office for the King's Cross route.

Canon Fellows has summarised the best timings between King's Cross and Cambridge after the Shepreth section was doubled in 1867. Originally the journey took 107min for the 58 miles in the down direction and 110min up. By 1880 the best times had been reduced to 80min down and (by an up train with only one stop at Hitchin) 75min. This enterprise was, however, not long-lived and the best times by 1883 were 77min down and up. Even so, over a longer route, this compared well with the GER performance, particularly taking into account the long uphill grind mostly at 1 in 200 for 12½ miles from King's Cross to Potter's Bar, for down trains.

Major accidents have been mercifully few on the Cambridge main line, though there have been too many minor incidents to list here. A bad one in the 19th century was at Tottenham on 20 February 1860, in Eastern Counties days. The 7.30am train to Cambridge was drawn by one of the E.B. Wilson 2-2-2s. Approaching the Hale station, one of the leading wheels of the engine lost its tyre; the locomotive and front carriages were derailed, hitting the station platform with catastrophic results. Fatalities included the driver, fireman and five passengers. The cause was a serious flaw in the weld of the tyre, which was wrought iron. Coincidentally, the accident was witnessed by Robert Sinclair, the ECR Locomotive Superintendent, who was standing on the station at the time. It was almost certainly in consequence of this that Robert Sinclair became one of the first locomotive engineers to make extensive use of steel for locomotive parts, especially tyres.

The Great Northern line saw serious accidents, eg at Welwyn Tunnel in 1866 and Hatfield in 1870, but these did not involve Cambridge line trains.

Turning to locomotive power, the most striking feature of the ECR and GER in the 19th century is the speed with which Locomotive Engineers (or Superintendents) were changed — no less than eight (six permanent and two interim appointments) up to 1899, compared with, for example, three on the GNR, three on the GWR and two on the Midland! Several reasons may have contributed to this: the GER's pay levels were lower than those of the Midland Railway and the North Eastern, whither S.W. Johnson and T.W. Worsdell respectively migrated. Also, the GER like the ECR before it, for a long time bought most of its engines from private building firms; only a minority were constructed at the railway's own Stratford Works, though after 1885, with better facilities, all new locomotives were built there apart from a batch of S69 (B12) 4-6-0s in 1920–21.

The best authority for the rather erratic locomotive history of the ECR and the GER until modern times is the late E.L. Ahrons, apart from an authoritative series of unsigned articles in the *Locomotive Magazine* between 1901 and 1913. Ahrons' encyclopaedic volume *The British Steam Railway Locomotive, 1825-1925* is supplemented by the records of locomotive performance in his famous 'Locomotive and Train Working in the Latter Part of the Nineteenth Century' articles for the *Railway Magazine*. These are less objective and authoritative, perhaps, than his major volume, because they depend on logs of train performance, some of his own and some sent him by correspondents, which must necessarily have been a random selection. But they are always illuminating, as are Ahrons' touches of humour or prejudice.

Turning to the locomotive designs actually employed: in Northern & Eastern days the services started with a batch of 2-2-2 inside cylinder engines from Robert Stephenson, Tayleur, Bury

Curtis Kennedy, and R.B. Longridge, a type very extensively used in the 1840s. Robert Stephenson also sold the Northern & Eastern one of their 'long boiler' engines, in which all three axles were placed under the boiler and in front of the firebox. The long overhang produced a certain amount of swaying at speed, but this design survived in different forms on a number of railways for many years.

The opening to Cambridge under Eastern Counties auspices was marked by the arrival of 20 locomotives from two builders, Jones & Potts, and Stothert & Slaughter, 10 from each firm, a mixture of 2-2-2 and 2-4-0 types. Later there came 10 4-2-0 engines from Jones & Potts. Some 'long boiler' types appeared on the Eastern Counties line, where Ahrons comments that they performed better than elsewhere owing to improved wheel balancing. (The Locomotive Superintendent of the ECR, W. Fernihough, pioneered the use of rim weights to balance the revolving and reciprocating masses.) Less satisfactory were three locomotives of the unique 'Crampton' type from the firm of E.B. Wilson. Five were built in 1848, with leading wheels 4ft 6in in diameter and 7ft drivers, but an intermediate pair of wheels of 3ft 6in in order to clear the cylinders. These, according to Ahrons, were the forerunners of the well-known Cramptons used on the Chemin de fer du Nord and other Continental railways.

That the ECR was, despite its poor financial situation, anxious to pioneer improvements in locomotive design is shown by its patenting of the principle of a compound engine in 1850 and the conversion of two existing locomotives to the compound principle, unfortunately without great success at that time. This lack of success is attributed by Ahrons to a general shortage of motive power on the ECR at the time which prevented extensive testing of two locomotives of experimental, if promising, unorthodox design.

The ECR had established locomotive repair shops at Romford but in 1848 these were moved to a larger site at Stratford, where many houses were built for the workers and the district was nicknamed 'Hudson Town'. For the first three years all locomotives continued to be bought from private firms, the Stratford Works concentrating upon repairs.

By 1851 J.V. Gooch had become Locomotive Superintendent and the Stratford Works had ceased to be used solely for repairs. Gooch is chiefly remembered for the express 2-2-2 tank engines with outside cylinders which he built for the ECR. They had 6ft 6in driving wheels and 110lb/sq in boiler pressure. Although these were built at Stratford, between 1855 and 1856 Gooch ordered 18 2-4-0 locomotives with 5ft 6in coupled wheels for goods work from Sharp Stewart, Kitson, and the Canada Works of Birkenhead. Finally Gooch designed some 2-2-2 tender locomotives much resembling his express tank engines of the same wheel arrangement.

In 1856 the Eastern Counties acquired from the Caledonian Railway Robert C. Sinclair as its Locomotive Superintendent. He is chiefly remembered for the well-known 'Sinclair singles', outside-cylinder 2-2-2 locomotives of elegant proportions, and also his 2-4-0 outside-cylinder goods engines built by no less than six manufacturers, including Schneider et Cie, in France, which also built a batch of 'singles' — the first British locomotives to be built abroad since the early 1840s. He was a strong advocate of outside cylinders. The passenger singles were credited with considerable speed capacity. Unfortunately they suffered a number of derailments, though not on the Cambridge main line. That may have been due to the slower running as compared with the Colchester line; they could however perform well on the level stretches of the Joint Line in later years.

Sinclair was succeeded in 1866 by Samuel Waite Johnson on the Great Eastern, as the ECR had by now become. His engines foreshadowed his later and more famous designs for the Midland Railway. Not surprisingly, his principal products were 2-4-0 and 0-6-0 types, with eventually a 0-4-4T largely intended for the various suburban services via the new Bethnal Green–Hackney Downs line after its opening in 1872. Johnson was as strong an advocate of inside cylinders as Sinclair had been of outside cylinders. Photographs of his engines could, from a distance, be taken for those of his later Derby products. His last gift to the GER was a pair of 4-4-0 inside-cylinder express passenger engines very similar to his graceful Midland express engines.

Johnson was followed in 1873 by William Adams; once more, outside cylinders became fashionable. Adams anticipated for the GER his LSWR 4-4-0 design, but with less success than he was later to have: the class was used primarily for fast goods work. He also inaugurated in Britain the 2-6-0 Mogul design, again with outside cylinders. Ahrons relates that these engines, which were intended for the heavy coal trains from Peterborough via March, although they could

steam well when in good repair, were unreliable owing mainly to problems with steam pipe joints. Consequently they did less effective work than the older Johnson 0-6-0s although the latter were of lower nominal power.

One good feature of Adams's short tenure of office was his provision of adequate protection for the enginemen, which compared very favourably with the skimpy shelter offered by Johnson's elegant cabs.

Massey Bromley, who followed Adams, had an even shorter tenure of office. But in the space of 3½ years he provided the GER with five 4-2-2 outside-cylinder singles, some of which were used on Cambridge line expresses. He also built sixty 0-4-4T engines for the suburban services and country branches, emanating from Stratford Works, plus 10 from E. & W. Hawthorn. Ahrons refers to 'the astonishing manner in which they could climb the Bethnal Green Bank out of Liverpool Street with fifteen and sixteen six-wheeled coaches, frequently without slipping'. Tragically, Bromley died in an accident on the Manchester, Sheffield & Lincolnshire Railway in 1884, when an engine broke a crank axle when travelling at speed near Penistone and the coaches (though not the engine) fell down an embankment. This came three years after his retirement from the GER — ironically too, since he had championed the automatic air brake on the GER and the accident's effects were exacerbated by the use of the non-automatic vacuum brake.

The last two 19th century Locomotive Superintendents of the GER were T.W. Worsdell (1882–1885) and James Holden (1885–1907). Worsdell only stayed three years *en route* to the North Eastern; but he carried on Bromley's policy of relying on Stratford Works for most, if not all, the new locomotive power the GER required, a policy taken to completion by James Holden. Worsdell's main contributions to design were a passenger 2-4-0 and a freight 0-6-0, the former apparently only moderately successful but the second class (which became the LNER 'J15' class) much more so. (Eventually, perpetuated by James and Stephen Holden and Alfred Hill, the class numbered 289 and was the most numerous inherited by the LNER in 1923.) Worsdell also introduced a tank engine, a 2-4-2T type, which lasted a long time in suburban service. His last legacies to the GER were the splendid Royal blue livery as standard, and 11 4-4-0 compound locomotives on the two-cylinder von Borries system which he was later to perpetuate extensively on the North Eastern. Ahrons wrote that 'Worsdell's compound locomotives were considerably simpler and cheaper to construct than Webb's three-cylinder type, and, within the writer's experience, their performances on the road were superior'.

James Holden, who followed Worsdell, remained at Stratford until 1907 and stamped his image on the GER almost as thoroughly as Churchward did on the GWR. Like Churchward at Swindon, he reorganised main workshops and built locomotives that could be perpetuated as standard work-horses for a long time to come. His first general-purpose passenger engine was the 'T19' 2-4-0, of which 110 were built, with only minor modifications between the various batches, over 11 years. These engines regularly served the Cambridge main line both from Liverpool Street and St Pancras.

Holden also built sound and reliable 0-6-0 freight engines and 2-4-2T locomotives for suburban and branch line work; but his chief achievements in the latter field were the extraordinarily efficient 0-6-0T engines that he produced in quantity from 1886 onwards, totalling 230 in all four classes. They tackled heavy suburban trains with gusto and eventually proved the backbone of the 'Jazz Service' introduced on 1920, when these little engines might have been considered life-expired. A.J. Hill built 30 more which were similar to Holden's apart from having rimmed chimneys and cabs with larger rectangular sides and high arched roofs.

Cambridge even after 1893 was accustomed to see locomotives of the 2-2-2 wheel arrangement which Holden had found suitable for the level stretches between Cambridge, Doncaster and York via the Joint Line. Holden continued for a time with single-drivers but eventually brought out his masterpiece, the 'Claud Hamilton' or '1990' class of 4-4-0, one of the classic British examples of this wheel arrangement, with 7ft-diameter driving wheels, inside cylinders and 180 lb/psi boiler pressure — an elegant and effective machine for all types of express passenger work. Ahrons, not given to excessive praise, wrote that the 'Claud Hamiltons' have done 'excellent work, often of a very exacting character'. The first of the 'Clauds' appeared in 1900, which may be considered either the last year of the 19th century or the first of the 20th; their exploits will therefore be discussed in the following chapter.

As far as the King's Cross route was concerned, the year in which the GNR regained control of the Hitchin–Shepreth line with running

A drawing of a Robert Sinclair 2-2-2 express passenger locomotive, as decorated for the Wedding Train of the then Prince of Wales. *North Woolwich GER Museum*

GER Johnson 4-4-0 No 305 captured at Liverpool Street in the 1890s. Note the 'Midland' look, but also the stovepipe chimney.
*National Railway Museum/Crown Copyright Reserved.*

powers to Cambridge (1866) was also the year when Patrick Stirling became Locomotive Superintendent of the Great Northern. Alas, it does not seem that any of his beautiful and legendary '8ft singles' ran to Cambridge — not, that is to say, before the 1938 runs by a replica 'Flying Scotsman' train of 1888, when No 1 emerged from the York Railway Museum in all its glory.

King's Cross to Cambridge services were not usually handled by purpose-built locomotives, but by engines cascaded from the main line. So, for a long time, after Stirling's arrival, Sturrock engines such as his 7ft 2-2-2s were used on the Cambridge expresses. Ahrons recalls that No 240A and No 229A of that class 'for many years maintained the Great Northern reputation on the London–Cambridge line for fast running'. In addition, Sturrock's 0-4-2 tender engines (rebuilt

in many cases by Stirling), as well as his 2-4-0 engines, were suitable for this line and were followed eventually by Stirling's own 2-4-0s ('secondary main line standard' Class E2) and 0-4-2 ('mixed traffics' of Class F2) well into the 20th century. Minor variations in design appeared in the various batches of these engines built between 1867 and 1896. Patrick Stirling died in harness, in 1895, at the age of 75, after 29 years in office. The work of his successor, H.A. Ivatt, really belongs to the 20th century.

# The Liverpool Street Story

Liverpool Street station in 1991 reached the last stages of a vast reconstruction scheme designed to make it finally a really modern and convenient terminus. Its history has been complicated. It was originally built (like Waterloo) as a replacement nearer to the city centre for an earlier, inconveniently remote, station. As explained in Chapter 1, the Northern & Eastern Railway's trains from the outset joined the Eastern Counties line at Stratford and used the ECR's terminus at Shoreditch, which itself replaced a temporary station that had been opened in June 1839 at Devonshire Street, Mile End. The ECR was extended in September 1840 to reach a rather more permanent site at Shoreditch just before the Northern & Eastern started running in from Stratford. It was built on the site of a slum known as Webb's Square, one of the dreadful 'rookeries' of early Victorian London.

The station was originally a poor affair with just two platforms and five tracks between them, served by one pair of lines from Stratford. Many complaints of its inadequacy were made. In 1847–8 better buildings were provided by the ECR's architect, Sancton Wood, together with more tracks, partly to provide for the Northern & Eastern trains, by now operated by the ECR.

In its final form, judging by contemporary pictures, it was not unimpressive, being built on arches with an Italianate façade and twin curving carriageways rising from street level. It had also (rather disingenuously) been renamed Bishopsgate in 1846, to give the impression of being less remote from the centre. Location was in fact its main drawback; a contemporary complaint was that 'few omnibuses ply to it, and most of the approaches to it are so narrow that it is difficult to reach it, even in cabs, without serious delay'. But despite this handicap, by 1863 the station was handling almost four million passengers a year, and it survived for a quarter of a century from its opening — far longer than Waterloo's predecessor, Nine Elms, on the London & South Western, which lasted only 10 years.

Replacing Bishopsgate was a long-drawn-out process. It was to some extent stimulated by the successful extension of the North London Railway from Kingsland into a new terminus with a frontage to Liverpool Street, well inside the City. The NLR secured an Act of Parliament in 1861 and opened its handsome new station called Broad Street in October 1865 with highly satisfactory results, the number of passengers over the line immediately doubling and thereafter increasing still further.

The Eastern Counties, handicapped by a weak financial position, considered building a link between its Cambridge line at Tottenham and the North London at Kingsland so as to divert part of its traffic into Broad Street, and actually deposited a bill for this purpose in 1862. The North London however objected and the House of Commons threw out the bill.

The Great Eastern, by then the successor to the ECR, produced in 1862 a scheme for a high-level line with a terminus at Finsbury Circus, which was rejected by Parliament; it was followed by yet another abortive proposal two years later for a high-level station, this time in Wormwood Street in the City, with an approach by a viaduct parallel with the North London line to Broad Street. Finally, in 1864 Parliamentary powers were obtained for a line leading to a station fronting Liverpool Street, adjacent to Broad Street, but still on a high level. The same Act authorised a new line from Bethnal Green to

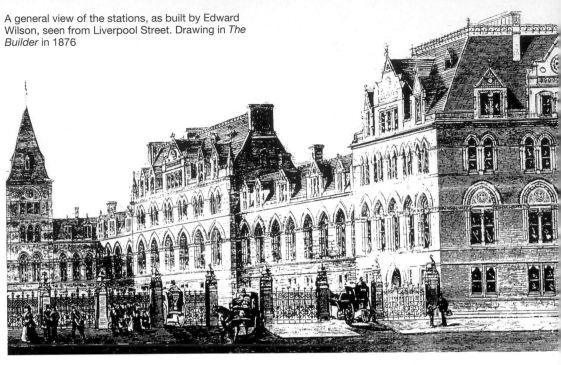

A general view of the stations, as built by Edward Wilson, seen from Liverpool Street. Drawing in *The Builder* in 1876

Edmonton and a branch from Hackney Downs to Walthamstow. This was to be followed by a chord line from Clapton Junction to Copper Mill Junction on Walthamstow Marshes, enabling the Cambridge line services to enjoy a shorter route than the original one via Stratford.

The Act took some cognizance of the hardship that construction of the Broad Street line had caused through the demolition of house property. It was now estimated that the Liverpool Street extension from Bethnal Green would involve the loss of 280 houses. As some amelioration, the Act required the railway to provide workmen's trains at a return fare of 2d (0.8p) between Liverpool Street, Edmonton and Walthamstow.

Obtaining Parliamentary powers was only the beginning of a long process that came to a virtual standstill for a time. It started quite well, under the direction of Robert Sinclair who (oddly, to present-day ideas) doubled the roles of Locomotive Superintendent and Civil Engineer for the GER. A main contractor, Lucas Brothers, was appointed and notices to treat were served on property owners along the route. These proved to include some important properties, such as the Worship Street Gas Works and the City of London Theatre, as well as a hospital. There were also numerous houses and small businesses needing to be acquired, at a total cost

much in excess of the original estimate. Meanwhile, the contractors were unable to start work and complained of the delay. Matters were further complicated by negotiations with the East London Railway, intended to give the ELR use of the basement of the GER terminus in return for sharing in the construction cost. Lastly, the financial crisis of 1866 hit the GER very severely and for a short time it was actually in the hands of the Receiver.

This hiatus lasted until 1870. The eventual recovery was marked by some important changes in personnel. Lord Cranborne, soon to succeed as Marquess of Salisbury, became Chairman in January 1867 and this helped to restore the GER's standing in the financial world. (He did not remain in the Chair for more than four years however, being followed by a less eminent figure, Lightly Simpson, who saw the Liverpool Street project take shape.) Shortly afterwards, in 1870, a new General Manager arrived in the person of Samuel Swarbrick from the Midland Railway; he had already been acting as a financial consultant to the GER, the field in which his chief abilities lay. Lastly, Robert Sinclair was replaced as engineer by Edward Wilson, coming from the Great Western, after a short period as an independent consulting civil engineer. Wilson's name is always associated with the design and construction of Liverpool Street. The

*Top:* The main line station in GER days, showing apparently Platform No 10 with spectators of some shunting movements. *Author's Collection*

*Above:* No 14, a GER J. Holden 4-2-2 stands awaiting release from a platform. *Locomotive & General*

TO THE
GREAT NORTHERN
RAILWAY STATION.

*Left:* A great contrast to Liverpool Street — the GER's so-called 'West End' terminus at St Pancras.
*British Rail*

*Above left:* The west suburban side of the concourse, showing the tearoom built out on stilts.
*North Woolwich GER Museum*

*Above right:* Simple train describer boards for Enfield and Chingford lines pictured in the pre-Grouping era.
*Author's Collection*

*Below:* The east side suburban platforms seen when services were operated by steam.
*H. C. Casserley*

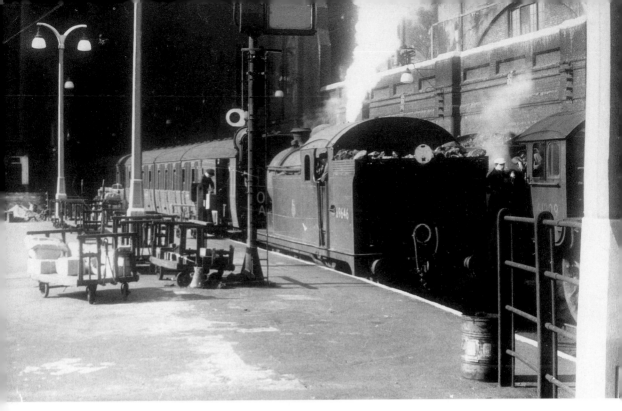

An Enfield-bound train pictured waiting to leave Liverpool Street in 1958. *R. M. Casserley*

Board thought so highly of him that by 1899 his salary was £3,000, a very large sum for those days.

Once the GER was out of Chancery, work on the Liverpool Street project resumed and — most significantly — in 1870 a new Act was obtained changing the route to a low-level one, making connections with both the East London Railway and with the Metropolitan Railway which was then extending eastwards from its original terminus at Farringdon Street. One may detect in this change of policy the influence of Sir Edward Watkin, a director of the GER but also Chairman of the Metropolitan as well as of the East London Railway. It is perhaps significant that Edward Wilson had been working since 1864 as a consulting engineer to the Metropolitan Railway for its extensions from Farringdon Street to Liverpool Street.

However, if Watkin was a main policy influence, the execution of the scheme seems to have been left to Swarbrick and Wilson. Lord Claud Hamilton, who was to become the GER Chairman in 1900, complained that as a Director he had been unable to influence or even obtain information about the Liverpool Street project, due to the then Chairman, Lightly Simpson, being dominated by Swarbrick. Swarbrick enjoyed a salary of £3,000 matching Wilson's,

until he 'left the service' (voluntarily or otherwise) in 1880. The politics of the Board Room at Bishopsgate must have been exciting, since Sir Edward Watkin was not easily dominated by anyone! Swarbrick's strength lay in finance, and it seems likely that he left Wilson to get on with all the detailed planning for the new station.

Wilson is an interesting figure, even more of a polymath than his predecessor, Sinclair, since he was not merely both a locomotive and a civil engineer, but also something of an architect. He had been Locomotive Carriage & Wagon Superintendent of the West Midland Railway (later the West Midland Section of the GWR) and also that line's civil engineer. But it would appear that he was brought in to the Great Eastern primarily to deal with Liverpool Street in all its aspects, since Sinclair's locomotive duties were taken over by S. W. Johnson from July 1866.

The decision to adopt a low-level route introduced a handicap which many generations of engine drivers and their firemen have cursed, namely the stiff gradient of 1 in 70 for half a mile

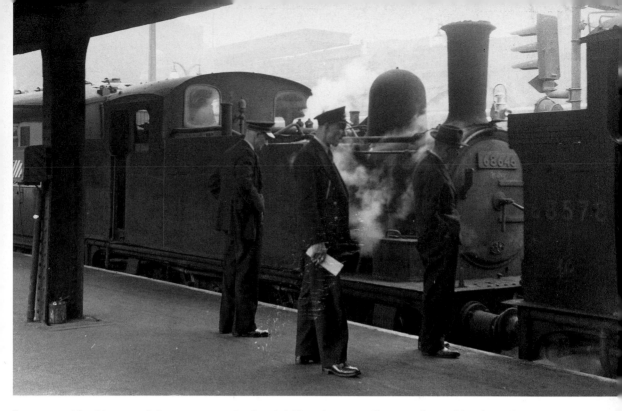

There is apparently a coupling problem here at Liverpool Street on 24 June 1956. *T. Middlemass*

from outside Liverpool Street up to Bethnal Green. This was caused by the need to build the station below street level, the access lines passing beneath Pindar Street, Primrose Street and Worship Street.

For a short time before the station was completed, trains used platforms built in November 1872 adjacent to but below the original terminus and named Bishopsgate Low Level. Some platforms remained in limited use until May 1916 and can still be seen when leaving the main station.

In addition to the gradient handicap, the planning of the station's layout was flawed. Wilson's design really comprised two stations under a single train shed. The main line station was based on a design that had been used for earlier stations such as Paddington and King's Cross, but was already obsolete and had been abandoned in more modern stations such as St Pancras (1868), Charing Cross (1864) and Cannon Street (1866). It provided only a single departure platform and a single arrival platform. Alongside the departure platform was a cab road with the booking office, waiting rooms and other facilities. Alongside the arrival platform there was another cab road, for passengers alighting from the trains.

This pattern was not unsuitable so long as only one departing and one arriving train had to

be handled at a time; it quickly became inadequate as the number of trains grew. (At Paddington and King's Cross the carriage stabling roads had already by 1870 been replaced by additional platforms.)

At Liverpool Street, unfortunately, a main line station very much on this traditional pattern was included, though with only two stabling roads between the departure and the arrival platforms. The main line tracks extended beyond the actual platforms into a sort of no man's land where they were connected by turntables for shunting short-wheelbase vehicles, as originally planned at Paddington and King's Cross.

A second station for suburban trains was sited alongside the main line station, though further away from the street-line. Each station had its own set of booking offices and concourse areas. Platforms 1 to 8 comprised the suburban station: Platforms 9 and 10 the main line station.

Outside the station, a connection with the East London Railway called Bishopsgate Junction was brought into use in April 1876. Another fea-

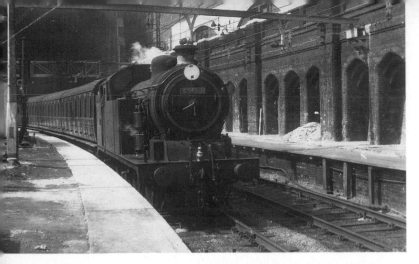

*Left:* On 2 July 1960, pending electrification, a typical suburban train of the period waits to depart. *H. C. Casserley*

*Centre left:* The 12.30pm service to Norwich pictured about to leave Liverpool Street on 14 August 1946. *R. M. Casserley*

*Bottom left:* A Gresley-designed Class K3 2-6-0 waits outside the station on 2 July 1960. *H. C. Casserley*

*Right:* 'Sandringham' class 4-6-0 No 61608 *Gunton*, stands with its train at Liverpool Street on 16 August 1958. *H. C. Casserley*

ture was that originally Nos 1 and 2 were through platforms, their tracks leading by means of a sharp curve to the Metropolitan Railway. Access to No 1 Platform from the concourse thus involved crossing by footbridge. However, the use of this connection never fulfilled the intentions of Sir Edward Watkin, although for a short time while the Metropolitan was being extended from Moorgate Street, pending completion of its own Liverpool Street Station, its trains ran round the curve into the main line station and terminated there. Watkin proposed a through service from the Metropolitan to the East London via Liverpool Street, but the GER traffic people sensibly vetoed this since it would have involved crossing all the tracks outside the station on the level. Thereafter the link was seldom used except for occasional excursion trains and it was finally removed in 1920, when the 'Jazz Service' was inaugurated and better access to Platform 1 than by a footbridge was needed.

On the other hand, the link with the East London Railway was used for a variety of suburban services. For instance, the South Eastern operated in the 1880s a service between Addiscombe Road and Liverpool Street, while the GER ran into New Cross. The London, Brighton & South Coast Railway ran between Liverpool Street and Crystal Palace for a time. Freight trains also used the connection despite having to reverse in the platforms at Liverpool Street — usually in the night-time, for obvious reasons. There was later a wagon hoist at Spitalfields (for Bishopsgate Goods) capable of holding two wagons at a time, constructed in 1900. Bishopsgate Junction was removed in 1966; the wagon hoist ceased to be used after 1955.

There was for a time an intention to make a connection from the East London Railway with the Cambridge line north of Bethnal Green, and a short length of tunnel under Bethnal Green was actually built for this purpose, though never completed or brought into use.

Liverpool Street's train shed, manufactured by the Fairbairn Engineering Company to Wilson's design, and covering both the main and suburban station, was unquestionably a fine and impressive structure of four spans, the two central ones being of 109ft and the outside flanking spans rather narrower. Alongside the main departure platform (No 9) a parallel building, with a short return to Liverpool Street, accommodated booking offices and waiting rooms for main line passengers at lower level whilst at street level and above, General Offices for the GER were provided.

*Above:* This view of Platform 9 shows the station pilot standing on the middle road, whilst a diesel shunter stands in Platform 10 with a parcels van. The electric wires have already arrived. *Author's Collection*

*Below:* Two engines wait to take water at Liverpool Street in March 1949.
*H. C. Casserley*

Wilson seems to have been his own architect for this building, constructed of white Suffolk brick coming from Lucas Brothers' brickworks at Lowestoft, with Bath stone facings. Its style has been described as 'typically mid-Victorian Gothic', but it had little of the flamboyance of Gilbert Scott's St Pancras Hotel. Arches were certainly pointed and the second floor windows were interestingly joined in pairs. There was originally ornamental ironwork on the roof giving a varied skyline.

Wilson's architectural merits have not on the whole been much praised. The erudite historian of London's termini, Alan Jackson, describes his work at Liverpool Street as having 'features seemingly taken from a copy-book of do-it-yourself architecture'. However, having myself worked in this building for some years, I can say that the interior was better than most railway offices; rooms were agreeably high and well-lit, corridors wide and staircases ample. It was, of course, like most buildings of its date, wasteful of space and expensive to heat.

At the north end of the building, where there was a return above the suburban concourse, Wilson provided a tower with a squat spire and a large clock.

The extent to which Wilson delegated any design work is uncertain; it was not until the last stages of construction that an architect, W.N. Ashbee, joined Wilson's staff; he was, later, to become the GER's Chief Architect.

Liverpool Street opened in stages during 1874, after which the old Bishopsgate became the GER's London Goods terminal — a rather imposing building for such a prosaic purpose. In modern times it was notorious for local working arrangements that made its goods handling costs excessive. There were few tears when it burnt down in the 1960s.

In a final judgement on Liverpool Street, one may well criticise the low-level strategy and the track layout of the station, but on the whole commend the office block and give unstinted praise to the train shed which has deservedly been made a Listed Building and splendidly restored as part of the 1992 reconstruction of Liverpool Street. It has been described as 'a highly refined version of the earlier Gare du Nord' but architectural opinion is even more flattering: 'the curves continue smoothly from one column to the next with almost weightless elegance'.

Particularly noteworthy is the delicate ironwork in the spandrels of the supporting columns, which has become visible again after decades of grime, picked out in contrasting colours. It ranks with other Victorian edifices in iron and glass which were promoted by the railway in days when there was a need to allow smoke and steam to rise and yet to afford passengers proper shelter from the weather. A final judgement is that Edward Wilson 'did what he could with an awkward site'.

The creator of Liverpool Street died in 1877, only three years after the station opened. But the site soon saw further developments. The first was the decision to build a major hotel, following the example of the Midland Grand at St Pancras and also the Charing Cross and Cannon Street hotels. The City of London was notoriously short of prestige hotels, apart from Cannon Street. The Board of the GER waited some time after 1874 for a suitable lessee to appear and eventually decided to build a hotel themselves. The architects were Charles Barry (son of Sir Charles Barry, the designer of the Houses of Parliament) and his son Charles Edward Barry, aged only 24 when this commission was accepted. (Charles Barry's brother, E.M. Barry, had built the Charing Cross and Cannon Street hotels.)

The hotel designed by the Barrys straddled the cab road leading down from Liverpool Street to the main line arrival platform, No 10. It comprised two blocks, described in *Building News* as being 'Early Renaissance in style, many of the details showing Netherlands influence'. The ground floor was in Portland stone, with red brick above. Internally, the hotel was luxuriously furnished by Maple & Co and it soon became popular, as eventually did the GER's restaurant car services which were supplied from the hotel.

One result of the construction of the Great Eastern Hotel was the covering in of the no man's land beyond Platforms 9 and 10. This extension of tracks was chiefly utilised (a colleague of mine once sardonically remarked) for the collection by wagon of loads of fish-heads from the hotel kitchen. To be fair, it was also a means of bringing in fuel for the hotel boilers, and permanent way materials for the engineers — a task performed by a 'ghost train' leaving Stratford around midnight. This small facility seemed quite unjustified in relation to the inconvenience caused by the separation of the main departure and arrival platforms, only connected by a footbridge, apart from the dark and tortuous exploration of passages known as the 'backs' under the hotel — a striking contrast to the gracious 'backs' of Cambridge!

*Above:* The Bethnal Green bank has always been associated with working into and out of Liverpool Street. A 'Britannia', No 70030, with exhaust shooting upwards, passes a 'B17', No 61651 *Derby County*, on 16 August 1958. *H. C. Casserley*

*Below:* 'Britannia' No 70001 *Lord Hurcomb* has just topped the bank with a Cambridge train on 16 August 1958. *H. C. Casserley*

*Top:* Class N7 No 69611, with a Chingford-bound train, is pictured arriving at Bethnal Green on 30 August 1958. *R. M. Casserley*

*Above:* A splendid collection of ex-GER lower-quadrant semaphores is seen at Bethnal Green awaiting postwar modernisation. *H. C. Casserley*

A misty morning at Bethnal Green West signalbox.
*H. C. Casserley*

The hotel itself could be entered from the station as well as from the street. Its buildings finally gave the station two quite impressive façades, to Liverpool Street and Bishopsgate. The hotel opened in May 1884; other developments were to follow. There was a vacant site left at the corner of Liverpool Street and Bishopsgate, between the end of the Great Eastern Hotel building and the new east side train shed. It was decided to use this for an extension to the hotel, largely designed for banqueting; the design was left to Maple & Co and that company's architect, Col R.W. Edis. The extension building, with its own entrance from Bishopsgate, was called the Abercorn Rooms, and incorporated two Masonic temples, one Egyptian, one Grecian, as well as other halls and banqueting rooms. It was opened in 1901.

The growth in traffic meanwhile had created a need for more platforms and more access lines. There was room on the east side, between the cab road along Platform 10 and Bishopsgate, for a new train shed accommodating eight platforms.

An Act of Parliament obtained in 1887 authorised the enlargement of the station. However, the conscience of MPs had been awakened to the problems of displaced people and the Act required the GER to rehouse 600 persons; it was calculated that 737 would be displaced. The Company built some unlovely tenement blocks for this purpose at Spitalfields, Whitechapel and Bethnal Green. (The LNER later sold them off in the early 1930s.)

The extension was designed by John Wilson, nephew of Edward Wilson, who had become the GER Chief Engineer in 1883. He was assisted by W.N. Ashbee who by now had become the company's Architect.

The train shed was less distinguished than that of the old station, consisting of a ridge-and-furrow glass roof covering both the platforms and a new concourse connected by a bridge (and later also a subway opened in 1912) to the older part of the station. The footbridge led past booking offices at street level to a Bishopsgate entrance, from which a staircase also gave access down to the concourse. The offices were in red brick, matching the upper floors of the hotel. The most attractive feature, though unfortunate-

'Britannia' class No 70002 *Geoffrey Chaucer* waits to leave Platform 9 at Liverpool Street with an express on 25 October 1960. *B. Wilson/The Gresley Society*

ly sited so high up as not to be noticed by most passengers, was a series of six delightful 'lunettes' in the brickwork, showing in relief cherubs acting as railwaymen — firing a locomotive, waving a guard's flag, pulling a signalbox lever, and so on. Fortunately, in the station reconstruction of the early 1990s some of them have been preserved and reinstated, though not on their original site.

With the construction of Platforms 11 to 18, and the addition of two more tracks up to Bethnal Green on the east side, major station reconstruction came to an end for many years; in fact from 1894 to 1960. But there were a good many less fundamental changes. In 1919 Sir Henry Thornton, the GER's dynamic American-born General Manager, was anxious to promote electrification of the suburban lines. The Board, however, jibbed at such an outlay, with the uncertainty about the Government's plans for the railway after the war and the ending of the wartime Control Period.

They opted instead for a reorganisation of the Enfield and Chingford line services devised by F.V. Russell, the Superintendent of Operation, which involved very quick turn rounds, made possible by providing engine docks at the outer ends of Platforms 1 to 4. An engine waiting there would move to couple up to the end of an arriving train almost before the latter had stopped. It would depart again within 4min, and the engine that had brought it in would move into the dock road, ready for the next arrival. At the busiest peak period, the interval between trains over the suburban line to Bethnal Green was only 2½min. Trains were speeded up and the first class portions were distinguished by a yellow stripe between the windows and the roof, the second class by a blue stripe; the object being to enable passengers to position themselves correctly on station platforms. This was responsible for the nickname 'Jazz Service' for what was officially described as 'The Last Word in Steam-operated Suburban Services'.

The tracks up to Bethnal Green were described as Suburban, Local, and Through. Roughly, the Suburban served the Hackney Downs route exclusively; the Local, both the Cambridge and Colchester lines; the Through,

solely the Colchester and Southend routes. Beyond Bethnal Green and as far as Hackney Downs the four tracks were known as the Slow and Fast Lines, only the former having platforms at the intermediate stations of Cambridge Heath and London Fields. (Incidentally, how incongruously rural are these names — Green, Heath, Fields, Downs — amid the East End's depressing jungle of bricks and mortar!)

Two features of Liverpool Street which older travellers remember are the huge 'Gothic' clock that hung from the roof in the western train shed, and the departure indicator with a battery of clock faces, set to show the departure times of trains whose destinations were displayed below on wooden slats.

Another, and very charming characteristic was the Edwardian-cum-Art Deco style of the tea-rooms situated on the footbridge. The one on the east side was converted into a stationmaster's office but the west side one survived until the present reconstruction, though in recent years becoming the 'Europa Bistro'. But whether drinking tea or eating a 'bistro' lunch, it offered customers an elevated view of the busy station concourse as a pleasant way to pass the time before or after a journey.

Changes came with electrification as far as Shenfield, opened in 1949, on the 1,500V dc overhead system. These trains ran from the east side of the station, and the electrification was associated with the construction of a flyover at Ilford which transposed the two eastern pairs of tracks. Hitherto it had always been an operating inconvenience that the 'Through' lines were on the east side, so that main line expresses to and from Platforms 9 and 10 conflicted with other services using Platforms 11 to 18. After 1949 the tracks were renamed Local, Main and Electric.

So far as the Cambridge line was concerned, Platforms 1 to 4 served Enfield, Chingford and (until its closure) the Palace Gates branch. Trains for Hertford, Bishop's Stortford, Loughton and Ongar used Nos 5 and 6; while 7 and 8 usually accommodated a Cambridge train, though in steam days Hunstanton and Norwich via

Cambridge trains with restaurant cars often, due to their length, shared the use of Platform 9 with Colchester line expresses. The Harwich boat trains, needless to say, were normally accommodated in Platforms 9 and 10, with No 11 also used in addition. Main line services for the Colchester, Clacton, Harwich and Southend lines were all seen in Platforms 11 to 18 as well as Ilford and Shenfield locals. Platform 9 did however condescend to accommodate some less important trains, the most conspicuous in the 1930s being the 6pm commuter 'express' headed by a 'J15' 0-6-0 goods engine, and incorporating three coaches for the Buntingford branch, a Gresley 'quad' articulated set for Hertford, three coaches for Bishop's Stortford and (until 1936) a slip carriage, detached at Waltham Cross. Such a train was a remarkable illustration of the Great Eastern's policy of providing through carriages to every possible destination — in many ways an admirable philosophy.

When electrification was being planned in 1955–60, there were some in the Eastern Region Planning Office who felt that the need to remodel the 'throat' area outside the station offered a golden opportunity to remove the longstanding inconvenience created by the division of the station. A track layout plan was prepared, enabling Platforms 9 and 10 to be extended at the 'country' end and correspondingly cut back at the bufferstop end, getting rid of the little-used stabling tracks between them and squeezing in an additional platform. Unfortunately, conservative elements in the operating department torpedoed this plan, arguing that the carriage stabling roads were still used, even if much less than formerly. However, the Planning Office on its own authority managed to cut back the projection under the hotel and at last in 1960 provide a walkway, even though a narrow one, between the two halves of the station.

Liverpool Street has always been a very important station for City workers who commute to and from their homes. Unlike Euston, Paddington, St Pancras, King's Cross or Victoria, it stands in the midst of banks and offices; the sleazy hotels which are to be found around several other London termini are much less in evidence here. One practice however grew up which the railway police had difficulty in stopping. Certain prostitutes would buy first class season tickets to Hackney Downs and in the late evening would accost 'City gents' taking trains that made that station the first stop. If they found a client, they would jump into an empty

*Left:* Class B2 No 61615 *Culford Hall* awaits departure time with a Cambridge Buffet Car express on 7 July 1953. *Author's Collection*

*Below left:* A 'Britannia', No 70039 *Sir Christopher Wren,* is about ready to depart with the 8.24am service for Norwich via Cambridge. *Brian Morrison*

*Right:* 'Re-united!' Romance could still exist in the murky atmosphere of the old Liverpool Street station. *C. R. L. Coles*

compartment with him before the train moved off on its 10min trip, leaving the (presumably) satisfied customer at Hackney Downs and returning to Liverpool Street by the next up train to resume their activities.

Today the old problems of 'The Street' — and the dedicated signalmen in the old West and East boxes who performed miracles of handling the intense peak-hour traffic with steam traction — are forgotten since a fine new station has emerged from the dust and chaos of the vast Broadgate development. Happily it incorporates, and in an extended form, the lofty and elegant arches of the western train shed which were the best feature of the original station. The office developments on the site of Broad Street and also that on a raft over the east side of Liverpool Street are lucrative enough to pay for the reconstruction of the station.

This scheme, funded by Rosehaugh Stanhope Developments, is one of the best examples of collaboration between British Rail and a private developer, not all of which have been so well conceived. New Street, Birmingham for instance, which has pushed the trains into a cellar, was a planning disaster from which Liverpool Street has been fortunately spared.

The separation of the hotel from the railway (in business terms if not physically) was enforced by a Government with no feeling for history or tradition; the Great Eastern Hotel had long served both City businessmen and tired travellers extremely well. Its catering was renowned and it was profitable to, in turn, the Great Eastern Railway, the London & North Eastern Railway and British Transport Hotels, its successive owners. Perhaps the highlight of its history was the banquet given on 15 July 1912 to celebrate the Golden Jubilee of the Great Eastern Railway. The menu consisted of nine courses, accompanied by the serving of two aperitifs, four wines including two champagnes and the superb Château-Lafite claret, followed by liqueurs and port 'in magnums'. This gargantuan feast of self-congratulation was presided over by the GER chairman, Lord Claud Hamilton, and attended by among others, the General Manager, Walter Hyde, who can have had no idea of the sword of Damocles hanging over him, leading to his enforced retirement in 1914 to make way for the dynamic American, Henry Worth Thornton.

Thornton, who had his own flat in the hotel, was one of many managers from the Great Eastern Railway, the London & North Eastern, and the Eastern Region of British Rail, who appreciated and used the excellent conference and dining facilities of the hotel. And to many travellers, especially from the Continent, arriving in the smoky cavern of Liverpool Street, the lit windows of the hotel overlooking the concourse were a welcoming sight. A pity that the link between railway and hotel was severed in an asset-stripping exercise directed against British Rail.

*Above:* Liverpool Street in sun and shade; the central tower stands truncated following bomb damage and the clock is a replacement of the GER original. *Author*

*Left:* Reconstruction has already started on the 'Broadgate' site, with Broad Street station no longer a neighbour of Liverpool Street. *Author*

*Above right:* The entrance to the reconstructed station, with the replica of the original clock tower duplicated. *Author*

*Far right:* The exterior of the Great Eastern Hotel — no longer railway-owned — pictured in 1992. *Author*

*Right:* The train departure indicator in the remodelled station. *Author*

The remodelled and restored block that formerly housed the GER (later the Eastern Region) head office. *Author*

The remodelled concourse showing the Bishopsgate (east) end. *Author*

# Twentieth Century Steam to Cambridge

The alternating phases of enterprise and stagnation, noted in the 19th century, continued in the 20th. Perhaps the halcyon period was the first decade and a half, culminating in the short-lived 'Radical Alterations' timetable of October 1914 which set standards of main line service previously unequalled on the GER. However, by the summer of 1914 the general standard of Great Eastern expresses had become quite respectable when compared with the mid-19th century. The weakness lay in the London suburban rolling stock, the 'dog-boxes' as Ahrons described many of the London commuter trains.

Two miscalculations led to unprofitable suburban extensions — on the Colchester line, the Hainault Loop from Woodford to Seven Kings and Ilford; and on the Cambridge line the Churchbury Loop, just over five miles long from Lower Edmonton to Cheshunt, with three intermediate stations, Churchbury, Turkey Street and Theobald's Grove. The competition from the electric trams which started running along the parallel main road in 1907/8 was so damaging that the Churchbury Loop lost its passenger trains in 1909. It was temporarily reopened in 1915 to provide transport for workers in munitions factories, but it closed again for passengers in 1919. The line remained open for a few freight services and as a diversionary route in the event of the main line being obstructed between Hackney Downs and Cheshunt. The station buildings were leased for various purposes, Churchbury becoming a joinery store. The eventual reopening of the Churchbury (renamed Southbury) line as part of the suburban electrification programme in 1960 is described in Chapter 12.

Returning to main line services and the early 20th century, by 1908 Cambridge had 11 up expresses over the GER line of which four were non-stop. The best trains were the 9.38am up breakfast car and the 5.12pm down dining car expresses. Journey times varied between 71 and 80min, including the St Pancras trains.

In those years Cambridge enjoyed through services to numerous destinations including Yarmouth, Hunstanton, Lowestoft, Wells-next-the-Sea, and Harwich (Parkeston Quay), not to mention the trains over the Joint Line to March, Lincoln and Doncaster. In fact, for a time in 1904 the best timings between London and Cambridge had been by the 11.05am and 4.30pm Liverpool Street to York trains.

The Great Eastern Railway tried hard to popularise what it described as the 'Cathedrals Route' — the cathedrals being Ely, Lincoln and York — with three daily through trains, one at 8.40am in addition to the two already mentioned. The youthful Cecil J. Allen, who lived at Clapton, but worked in the Resident Engineer's office at Broxbourne, used to catch a train in the morning back to Liverpool Street in order to travel in luxury by the 8.40am to his office at Broxbourne.

In later years these York services declined, being largely maintained for the benefit of the parcels traffic, hopes of persuading passengers to use the Joint Line by the sound of cathedral bells having faded.

Although the Great Northern could, in terms of mileage and route, compare very effectively for the London–Cambridge traffic, it did so only spasmodically. It was after all just a branch line service in the eyes of managements concerned with the East Coast main line and the West Riding. Moreover, the Great Eastern could reduce any advantage in terms of location accruing to King's Cross by running into St Pancras. The whole relationship of course was changed at

A down goods train seen passing Cheshunt during LNER days. *Real Photos*

the Grouping, though a few St Pancras services lasted until the LNER management got round to eliminating this trace of GER practice.

Nevertheless, in the first decade or so of the 20th century, as Professor Jack Simmons relates in his splendid book on St Pancras Station, higher academic circles at Cambridge preferred the Great Northern route for visits to London, King's Cross being a more acceptable station at which to arrive than either of the alternatives.

The King's Cross trains in these years usually numbered about eight down and seven up, all calling at Hitchin, with the best journey time no more than 75min. By 1912, Cambridge was linked to three London termini with a total of no less than 40 trains.

The GER main line rolling stock, largely clerestory-roofed with interior 'Lincrusta' panelling, rode reasonably well, though the Great Eastern's permanent way could not compare with that of , say, the London & North Western. The restaurant car services were excellent, maintaining a standard set by the Great Eastern Hotel under its redoubtable manager, Mr Amendt.

On the Cambridge line some restaurant cars ran only as far as Ely, where they would be detached and return with an up train. In view of the number of passengers making connections at Ely, this was a sensible practice. Because of the

relatively short runs between main stations on the GER also, the restaurant car staff were experts at quick service. I can recall in later years being served a four-course dinner between Bishop's Stortford and Liverpool Street!

However, this train service did not satisfy the dynamic 41-year-old Henry Worth Thornton when he arrived, sponsored by Lord Claud Hamilton, early in 1914 from the Long Island Railroad to become General Manager of the GER. Not only did he dispel the last traces of Eastern Counties parsimony by raising salaries (something ex-GER managers had to pay for after 1923 when they became part of the London & North Eastern) but he set up a committee to overhaul the timetable. Surprisingly, this committee was chaired not by an operator but by H.W. Firth, the GER's Electrical Engineer. It was of course the case that Thornton's long-term aim, based on his USA experience, was electrification of the GER, at any rate of the suburban services. Meanwhile, he was determined to push steam traction to its limits. The Firth committee produced a plan which Thornton accepted, and the timetable for

An up goods at Cheshunt hauled by 'J65' 0-6-0 No 8214 in 1939. *C. R. L. Coles*

October 1914, issued in a stiff blue cover, is now a collector's piece. It stated in bold type:-

SPECIAL NOTICE

THESE TIME TABLES INCLUDE MANY <u>RADICAL ALTERATIONS</u>

IN THE MAIN AND BRANCH LINE SERVICES

Thornton's 'radical alterations' were most drastic on the Colchester line. On the Cambridge line it was higher frequency rather than greater speed that was striking. A train prominently marked in the timetable as 'FAST TRAIN TO DONCASTER AND YORK', the 8.52am (non-stop to Cambridge) arrived in York at 2.9pm (5hr 17min later), 317min for 215 miles. But there were now 15 down expresses from Liverpool Street to Cambridge daily and three from St Pancras. Of the Liverpool Street trains, five were non-stops, though previous non-stop runs from St Pancras disappeared. This compared with the previous 10 ex-Liverpool Street and five from St Pancras, of which five had been non-stop. (Evidently paying tolls to a foreign line did not appeal to Thornton.) These changes gave a best London-Cambridge timing of 71min; they also gave much better connections to many branches. Earlier up (5.13am compared with 8.40am) and later down (11.30pm compared with 10.7pm) services made daily commuting from Cambridge easily practicable, for the first time.

It was sad that, in common with the other main line companies, the GER had to reduce and slow down its express train services during World War 1. In fact the Thornton 'Radical Alterations' timetable was never fully restored.

After the war, quite early in the 1920s, the LNER as successor to the GER began to experience competition from motor coaches. Cambridge and London were linked by two operators, Varsity Express Motors and Westminster Coaching Services. Most of the coaches went beyond Cambridge to points such as Ely, Bury St Edmunds, Wisbech or Norwich, providing roughly an hourly frequency on the London–Cambridge section of the route.

This competition was sharpened by the cheapness of the fare compared with rail, and also the convenience of running to and from the centre of Cambridge. Both these services were later bought up by the Eastern Counties Omnibus Company in which the LNER had a big shareholding. That did not prevent the railway from appearing before the Licensing Authority (Traffic Commissioners) set up under the 1930

*Top:* A local terminating train pictured at Cheshunt. The date of this photograph is unknown. *T. Middlemass*

*Above:* An LNWR goods train leaves Bletchley *en route* for Cambridge headed by No 1020 *Majestic* c1918. *F. W. Goslin/The Gresley Society*

*Above: Claud Hamilton* stands resplendent at St Pancras in GER days in a beauty contest with the products of Derby. *North Woolwich GER Museum*

*Below:* A small-boiler Ivatt Atlantic pictured on a Cambridge express shortly after the 1923 Grouping. *Locomotive & General*

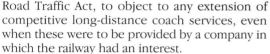

*Left:* Bishop's Stortford station c1910. *National Railway Museum/ Crown Copyright Reserved*

*Below left:* Class V1 2-6-2T No 447 pictured on a down stopping train near Broxbourne in 1938. *C. R. L. Coles*

*Right:* No 8792, clean and polished, stands at King's Lynn shed on 30 June 1936. *H. C. Casserley*

Road Traffic Act, to object to any extension of competitive long-distance coach services, even when these were to be provided by a company in which the railway had an interest.

In the last prewar summer, 1939, the fastest Liverpool Street–Cambridge train was the Thursdays only 11.10am buffet car express taking 65min non-stop. Most trains now called at Bishop's Stortford and Audley End, taking about 75min or a little longer. The famous 'Flying Fornicator', as it was known to undergraduates, 11.50pm on Thursday nights (the cheap return ticket day) took 71min. In my undergraduate days it had usually been hauled by an elderly J. Holden 2-4-0 and composed of six–wheeled carriages which racketed about on the curves leading to and from the Elsenham summit. The allowance of 25min from Bishop's Stortford to Cambridge was actually the fastest point-to-point timing on the ex-GER system.

The best up trains were the 8.45am buffet car train taking 66min, followed by the 9.7am which started from Hunstanton with a restaurant car. However, calling at Bishop's Stortford, it took 76min, a stately progress averaging 44mph, slower than the Norwich expresses via Cambridge had managed almost a century earlier. The regular time of 64 min for the Cambridge–King's Lynn run (just under 40mph over a level road) was lethargic.

In some ways the LNER showed most enterprise by reinvigorating the Great Northern route with the introduction of four 'Garden Cities and Cambridge' buffet car expresses in each direction calling at Welwyn Garden City, Hitchin and Letchworth, and taking about 77min or slightly less. Known as the 'Beer Trains', they were popular with undergraduates (and dons!) because King's Cross was nearer the West End than Liverpool Street. The popularity of the 'Beer Trains' is shown by the fact that they were planned as light three-coach sets but soon had to be lengthened to five coaches — and on Saturdays occasionally loaded up to 10, taxing the capacity of the old Ivatt 'Atlantics' diagrammed to work the service. In 1934 these trains departed at 9.25am, 12.30pm, 3.30pm, 5.25pm and 10.10pm from Cambridge — a fine proof of the maxim that 'facilities create traffic'.

In the brief rule of steam after World War 2, the chief event was the introduction in 1949 of a named daily express, the 'Fenman', leaving at 4.30pm (later 4.36pm) and running originally non-stop to Cambridge in 68min *en route* for Hunstanton — not a very brilliant piece of locomotive work. It went through several timing adjustments before diesel power arrived at the beginning of the 1960s.

Something must be said about the straggling cross-country route by the former London & North Western Railway from Cambridge via Bedford to Bletchley. About eight trains a day in the 1930s pursed a lethargic progress over this line, calling at all stations to Bedford and thereafter running fast to Bletchley in about 1hr 40min. Intermediate stations, Bedford to Bletchley, were served by their own independent service. As a means of travelling to the North-West, the Bletchley route had little attraction; in 1934 the quickest time from Cambridge to Crewe was 4¼ hr.

In theory, this route could have offered a through service between the two oldest universities and perhaps promoted 'cultural exchanges'

since the layout of the Bletchley junctions was suitable for through Oxford–Cambridge working without reversal. Connections were however not very good and it was a standing joke in both universities that 'cultural exchanges' often had to be effected in the waiting room at Bletchley. Sporadic attempts were made from time to time to organise things better but patronage was usually inadequate. In 1934 there was only one Oxford–Cambridge through train. The LMS experimented briefly in the 1930s with a three-coach diesel-electric unit which appeared for a time on the Oxford and Cambridge line; had it been promoted with the same enthusiasm as the Great Western was showing for its AEC diesel railcars, it might have stimulated enough traffic to become a permanent feature.

There is not much to be said about the Cambridge–Kettering service, because the LMS seemed to have little interest in developing it as a route to the north. About four trains a day (occasionally six) in each direction, stopping at all stations was the maximum; connections with Midland line expresses at Kettering were usually poor.

On its ex-GER country branches the LNER showed little of the spirit evident in other parts of the system. The drive of 'Punctuality Parkes' and Henry Thornton seemed to have been dissipated after the Grouping. The Mildenhall branch had just four trains daily each way; the cross-country line to Mark's Tey (for Colchester) had only one train that performed the 46½ mile journey in less than 2hr.

Use of the Cambridge line for Royal specials continued in the 20th century; King George V shared his father's liking for the bracing climate and the sporting facilities of the Sandringham estate — as indeed did his son, King George VI. Stanley Jenkins suggests that Sandringham House itself may not have been so healthy; certainly, no less than four Royal funerals started from it — the Duke of Clarence, Queen Alexandra, George V and George VI. After 1923

Royal specials starting from or arriving in London used King's Cross, which was just as convenient as St Pancras and was now under the same ownership as Liverpool Street. The Royal trains when passing Cambridge usually did not use the platform lines but the outside through tracks, which simplified security arrangements. A special drivers' 'Royal Link' was formed for this ex-GN and ex-GE combined route; the locomotive power was provided until the early 1930s by a pair of 'Super-Clauds' Nos 8783 and 8787 kept in spotless condition. They had a fixed turn of duties when not required for a 'Royal'. The King's Lynn–Wolferton short trip was entrusted to Nos 8792 and 8868. Eventually, about 1945, a 'B2', *Manchester City*, became Royal engine at Cambridge, being renamed *Royal Sovereign*. The spare 'Royal' engine was 'B2' No 1617, *Ford Castle*.

As regards freight on the Cambridge line, in addition to the heavy traffics such as household coal for London and export goods for the docks via Temple Mills, there was a considerable perishable market garden traffic from both the Spalding area and the Lea Valley. Cambridge had a number of light industries and an important jam-making centre at Histon. Express freight was promoted as early as 1906 by the institution of a Spitalfields–Doncaster fully fitted express limited to 25 vans and timed at passenger train speeds. The main factor in operation over the Cambridge line was of course the opening by the LNER of the two mechanised marshalling yards at March, 'Whitemoor Up' in 1929 and 'Whitemoor Down' in 1933. Whitemoor to Temple Mills was a major flow and although Cambridge was a staging point for recessing freights out of the way of passenger trains, and had its own inwards and outwards goods facilities, not much marshalling was done there.

South of Cambridge, line capacity was often taxed. Sometimes a total of 75 trains in a day's work had to be passed over the double line which only became four tracks for the short section below Pickett's Lock, half-way between Ponder's End and Angel Road. At various later dates, freight recessing facilities were provided by a small yard on the up side at Broxbourne and loops at Harlow, Spellbrook, Littlebury and Whittlesford.

As regards locomotive power, two of Sinclair's 2-2-2s were rebuilt as 4-2-2s. These, together with the unrebuilt 2-2-2s and also the Bromley singles, did not survive into the 20th century. By then the Sinclair outside-cylindered 4-2-2

*Left:* A Class B12 4-6-0, working on an up 'Garden Cities and Cambridge' express, is seen passing Hadley Wood in 1939. *C. R. L. Coles*

*Below left:* 'Claud Hamilton' class No 8783 — one of the two 'Royal' engines — is caught heading an up Cambridge express near Potter's Bar in 1938. *C. R. L. Coles*

*Top right:* Waltham Cross station pictured in pre-electrification days; dull, but typical of the Lea Valley section of the main line. *Author's Collection*

*Centre right:* An illustration of Audley End — then the junction for the branch to Saffron Walden — which shows the staggering of the platforms as the 2.24pm Liverpool Street–Norwich service passes. *H. C. Casserley*

*Bottom right:* Audley End station seen after its facelift, but before electrification. The famous *porte-cochère* is, however, not being used by Lord Braybrooke's carriage but by a commuter's motorcar. *Author*

*Above left:* An up stopping train pictured near Roydon in 1939 headed by 4-4-0 No 8876.
*C. R. L. Coles*

*Left:* A Cambridge line express passes Bethnal Green in the post-Grouping era. *Author's Collection*

*Above:* An up freight train caught near Roydon with an unidentified 'Austerity' 2-8-0 providing the motive power. *C. R. L. Coles*

'Greyhounds', as well as the Worsdell compounds, had been put out to grass, as it were, on the long level stretches of the Joint Line. Cambridge shed (or sheds) around 1908 had a total complement of 84 engines — the vast majority being of course GER, though the total included four from the GNR, two from the Midland, and a solitary one from the London & North Western.

Until Gresley arrived in 1923, mainstay of the Cambridge services was the 'Claud Hamilton' 4-4-0s and the '1500' series 4-6-0s, which were liked by the civil engineers for their low axle-loading and by their crews for their sheltering cabs with side windows, their good riding and general performance. As late as the end of the 1920s I well recall an up Hunstanton express arriving in Cambridge behind a 'Claud' that had brought it from Lynn, changed for a '1500' to carry on to Liverpool Street. The same sight is recalled by Richard Hardy as late as 1946–47.

After the 'Swedey' (as the GER was tagged) had been merged in the Southern Area of the LNER in 1923, Doncaster designs began to infiltrate. Some ex-Great Northern 'K2' 2-6-0s appeared on Cambridge trains, a prelude to the B17 'Sandringham' class of 4-6-0s designed by Gresley, the first of which was built in 1928, eventually Nos 2800 to 2872. They tended to be rough-riding, as I can testify from a footplate trip; but by and large they fitted the bill, and Cambridge shed looked after them well with double-manning.

Interestingly to the student of locomotive history, at Cambridge as late as the 1950s one could still see examples of LNER 'E4' 2-4-0s at work, which had been built by J. Holden in the 1890s and were the last class of 2-4-0 to work in Britain. They suited the Cambridge–Colchester line very well.

111

The 4.15pm train from Liverpool Street pictured during LNER days with a 'Sandringham' in charge. *Author's Collection*

Ex-'WD' 2-10-0 No 73788 heads an up goods service
at Cambridge on 14 July 1945.
*D. A. Dant/The Gresley Society*

Early in the 20th century King's Cross–
Cambridge trains were still sometimes 'horsed'
by 2-4-0 engines built by Patrick Stirling and
classed 'E2', the earliest dating from 1867 and
the last 1895. Some were rebuilt by H.A Ivatt.
Later came the Ivatt 'J' class 4-4-0s, useful general-purpose machines, followed by the small-boil-
ered Atlantics, otherwise called the 'Klondykes',
of which the prototype *Henry Oakley* has been
preserved. When Gresley's Pacifics took over the
main East Coast and West Riding expresses, the
large-boilered version of the Ivatt Atlantics that
had performed such magnificent feats with huge
loads during World War 1 were cascaded to secondary duties and they figured largely on the
Cambridge line, especially the 'Beer Trains'. In
1934 no less than five were shedded at
Cambridge, displacing the elderly 'Klondykes'.

A short-lived phenomenon after the 1923
Grouping was the appearance of some ex-GER
engines on the King's Cross route, both 'Claud
Hamiltons' and '1500' 4-6-0s, not solely on Royal
trains.

BR Standard locomotives began to replace
LNER types in the 1950s, but it was some time
before Cambridge saw 'Britannias', and then not
on the Hunstanton expresses, not even on the
'Fenman'. When the 4-6-2s began performing so
well on the Liverpool Street–Norwich line, a limited amount of 'triangular' working was instituted with some outward duties via Colchester
returning via Cambridge, and vice versa. In 1953
there were four such workings, all stopping at
Audley End and Bishop's Stortford — except that
on Sundays the 6.25pm from Norwich ran non-
stop from Ely to Liverpool Street. (Only
Newmarket race specials and Royal trains normally passed Cambridge without stopping.)

So far as 'foreign' lines were concerned, visitors to Cambridge over the ex-LNWR route from
Bletchley comprised a surprising variety of classes, from Webb 'Cauliflower' 0-6-2Ts and 2-4-2Ts
to the handsome 'Precursor' 4-4-0s and the even
larger 'Prince of Wales' and 'Experiment' 4-6-0s
after they had been downgraded from main line
express work.

In the last years of the LMS before nationalisation, Cambridge saw examples of the H.G. Ivatt
2-6-0 designed for secondary services. It is possible that engines designed by the two Ivatts,
father and son, might have occasionally stood
together, at opposite ends of Cambridge station.
After Nationalisation and until closure, the line
was often served by a very similar design, the BR
Standard mixed-traffic 2-6-0 with its strong LMS
parentage.

*Top:* A 'Claud' fitted with the larger boiler, No 2558, stands at King's Cross on 15 April 1947; wartime grime is still apparent. *H. C. Casserley*

*Above:* One of the least imposing of the Lea Valley stations, Angel Road, photographed prior to electrification. *Author's Collection*

*Above:* Brimsdown pictured during the steam era — another rather featureless station on the Lea Valley section. *Author's Collection*

*Below:* A Class D16 4-4-0 is pictured at the front of an up Cambridge express near Burnt Mill — a station now rebuilt and renamed Harlow Town — in 1947. *C. R. L. Coles*

*Above:* A stopping train for Liverpool Street is seen leaving Audley End tunnel on 26 August 1953. *L. R. Peters/The Gresley Society*

*Below:* Class B17 4-6-0 No 61600 *Sandringham* approaches Bishop's Stortford on 27 April 1952 with a Liverpool Street–Cambridge express. *Brian Morrison*

*Above:* 'Britannia' No 70003 *John Bunyan* comes off the north curve at Ely with an express from the Midlands to Yarmouth in August 1961. *John C. Baker*

*Below:* 'Britannia' class No 70037 *Hereward the Wake* — a highly appropriate name for the line serving Ely — passes Harlow on 1 June 1956 with a Cambridge–Liverpool Street express. *H. C. Casserley*

*Above right:* An Ivatt Class 2MT 2-6-0 enters Bartlow station on 27 April 1958 with the 4.2pm local from Cambridge to Mark's Tey. *Brian Morrison*

*Below right:* 'B17' No 61631 passes Angel Road station on 29 April 1951 with the 12.15pm Ely — Liverpool Street service. *John F. Ayland*

*Above left:* The 2.24pm service from Liverpool Street to Hunstanton is pictured leaving Ely on 25 June 1958. R. C. Riley

*Left:* A freight hauled by Class J17 No 65549 passes the famous 'triple distant' bracket signals outside Ely on 26 April 1958. *R. C. Riley*

*Top:* A Colchester-bound train stands in the bay at Cambridge station awaiting departure on 27 May 1957. *R. M. Casserley*

*Above:* The 3.21pm King's Cross–Ely train seen at Barnwell Junction, north of Cambridge, on 25 June 1958. *R. C. Riley*

*Above left:* A King's Lynn departure for Ely via March is hauled by 'Claud' No 62566 on 23 June 1958. *R. C. Riley*

*Left:* No 62610, a large-boilered 'Claud' enters King's Lynn on 23 June 1958 with the 8.24am departure from Liverpool Street. *R. C. Riley*

*Above:* Shelford station is pictured, looking towards Cambridge in May 1957. *R. M. Casserley*

*Centre right:* Class J39 No 64776, heading an up freight, emerges from Audley End tunnel on 5 August 1953. *L. R. Peters/The Gresley Society*

*Right:* An up express, headed by a 'Britannia' Pacific, regains open air on departure from Audley End tunnel on 11 August 1953. *E. R. Wethersett/Ian Allan Library*

*Left:* The cared-for station pilot at Liverpool Street blows off steam whilst awaiting its next duty. *Author's Collection*

*Centre left:* Bishop's Stortford station recorded in 1958. *Author's Collection*

*Bottom left:* A 'Britannia' Pacific, No 70002 *Geoffrey Chaucer*, carries the 'Fenman' headboard on a working of the express on an unknown date. *L. D. Peters/The Gresley Society*

*Right:* No 70007 *Coeur de Lion* heads a down Norwich service via Cambridge at Chesterton Junction on 28 August 1953. *L. R. Peters/The Gresley Society*

*Bottom right:* Class B17 No 61643 heads the 'Fenman' at Trumpington on 31 August 1951. *D.A. Dant/The Gresley Society*

*Left:* A stopping train is seen arriving from Bishop's Stortford at Audley End on 30 June 1951. *H. C. Casserley*

*Centre left:* A freight train emerges into daylight from Audley End tunnel behind a sturdy Class O1 2-8-0 on 19 July 1958. *Ken Nunn Collection/LCGB*

*Below:* Climbing the 1 in 70 Bethnal Green bank on 4 June 1958, 'Britannia' No 70007 *Coeur de Lion* powers the 5.54pm Liverpool Street–Norwich via Cambridge train as it overtakes the Class N7 0-6-2T labouring up the incline with an Enfield train. *Brian Morrison*

# Cambridge in Wartime

A first casualty of World War 2 was the rail passenger timetable. The first three weeks of the war showed a savage reduction of services, due to the expected immediate start of bombing. When this did not appear, a more rational set of Emergency Timetables was issued on 2 October 1939, which reflected speed restrictions and reduced frequencies. Between Liverpool Street and Cambridge, there were on weekdays only five down trains and five up trains that could be called 'expresses' in any way. Taking, typically, 1hr 35min with three stops, they achieved overall speeds of about 36mph. Shades of the Eastern Counties Railway! Other trains, calling at all stations north of Broxbourne took anything between 2hr 5min and 1hr 50min.

Using the King's Cross route offered no help. Changing at Hitchin with services between there and Cambridge 'all stations', the total journey could take between 2hr (by the 7am from King's Cross) to no less than 3hr 35min by the 9am. Average speeds between 29mph and 16mph!

These drastic cuts in passenger train services (later somewhat ameliorated) reflected the LNER's conviction that free movement of freight was essential to winning the war. The LNER was more involved with freight as a proportion of its total business than any other of the Big Four railway companies and its policy in wartime was to divert locomotives and crews from passenger work to freight, as well as restricting passenger paths in the timetable.

By contrast, the Southern Railway which had derived three-quarters of its traffic receipts from passengers maintained a wartime service far more comparable with what it had provided its customers in peacetime.

But if Cambridge lost on the passenger side, on the freight side it became even more of what George Hudson, 100 years earlier, had planned — a component in a great trunk route. Supplies and munitions flowed north and south to and from the Joint Line, and via Peterborough or via Bletchley, east and west through Cambridge.

The construction of airfields in East Anglia, largely for the use of the United States Army Air Force, produced major new flows of traffic passing via Cambridge. These included bricks from Bedfordshire, cement from various sources, rubble from bombed buildings, slag and tarmac. Most of these traffics moved in trainloads and often came by unusual routes compared with prewar practice. After the airfields were operational, trains of tank wagons loaded with aviation spirit became common. There were daily trains from Avonmouth into East Anglia via Didcot, Oxford, Bletchley and Cambridge.

Munitions — shells and bombs — also passed in huge quantities. Prewar, no more than five wagons of explosives could, by regulations, be included in any freight train: now the rule was relaxed to allow up to 60 wagons of explosives on Government account, and the maximum permissible load in each wagon was quadrupled. The old, quaintly named gunpowder vans were supplemented for this traffic by ordinary open (sheeted) wagons and covered vans.

Trains of munitions became so common that the railwaymen working them accepted the inevitable element of danger philosophically. Their attitude could indeed become heroic, as in the case of the accident at Soham in Cambridgeshire. The story has been told more than once, how on 2 June 1944 Driver B. Gimbert and Fireman J. Nightall were taking an ammunition train past Soham when the driver saw that the first wagon behind the tender of his 'Austerity' 2-8-0 was on fire. He stopped carefully and his fireman went back to uncouple the first wagon from the rest of the train. Gimbert then drew slowly forward, intending to take the wagon clear of the built-up area of Soham and then leave it standing uncoupled. Sadly, it exploded in the station, making a huge crater; but it did not set the rest of the train on fire and the village of Soham was saved from the destruction that must have followed in that event. Nightall was killed, as was the station signalman; Gimbert was seriously injured. Both enginemen were awarded (posthumously in Nightall's case) the George Cross, and have had locomotives named after them.

A wartime task for the Cambridge District office was setting up ambulance trains from coaches provided by all four of the main line railways. In total, eight trains of 16 coaches each were sent out to France but there do not seem to be precise records of what eventually happened to them.

Cambridge was spared the severe air bombardment on some other cities such as York in the so-called Baedeker List of targets. But services were disrupted from time to time. In particular, the line to Liverpool Street was badly blocked by damage at London Fields on 7 September 1940. The Cambridge line was used on occasion to avoid bomb damage between Stratford and Bethnal Green, trains travelling via Hackney Downs to Tottenham and reversing there. Liverpool Street itself was hit by bombs on Platforms 1 and 4. The General Offices were badly hit in the severe raid of 10–11 May 1941, which brought down much of the clock tower. The Great Northern route was also subjected to severe bomb damage at King's Cross and elsewhere.

Wartime freight movements brought many strangers to Cambridge including Stanier 2-8-0s, followed by the 'WD' standard 2-8-0s and the American-built 2-8-0s. A harassed shedmaster never knew what would arrive nor where it would end up after it left his care.

Left: Whitemoor Marshalling Yard; the Control tower of the up yard, from which countless freight trains were despatched through Ely and Cambridge throughout the years of World War 2. *British Rail*

Above: March station is situated on the main route from Cambridge to the industrial Midlands and North of England.
*Author's Collection*

Centre right: The locomotive manned by Driver Gimbert and Fireman Nightall pictured after the Soham explosion of 2 June 1944.
*D. A. Dant/The Gresley Society*

Below right: A view, in April 1946, which shows the Cambridge 'dump' of scrap metal and surplus locomotives.
*L. D. Peters/The Gresley Society*

*Above:* The 'Starving Lion' logo came to Cambridge after Nationalisation, but after a few years it was replaced by the more heraldic lion brandishing a wheel and eventually by the long-lasting BR double arrow. *British Rail*

*Below:* A slightly smartened-up 'Claud' is pictured at Ely on 25 August 1950. Although Nationalised, the locomotive is apparently lacking a BR logo on its tender. *H. C. Casserley*

# Nationalisation, Reorganisation, Rationalisation!

Cambridge, in common with other major British Railways centres, has experienced the effects of that ancient Chinese curse 'May you live in interesting times'. When on 1 January 1948 the London & North Eastern Railway ceased to own the Cambridge line, it was succeeded by the British Transport Commission, but for actual management purposes by the Eastern Region of the Railway Executive, a component of the BTC. At Cambridge itself not much changed overnight so far as organisation was concerned, since the Eastern Region in effect was the former Southern Area of the LNER. District Officers on the operating, loco running and commercial sides remained in and around Cambridge station and still responded to chiefs at Liverpool Street.

However, after a change of Government in 1951 and the abolition in 1953 of the Railway Executive, there followed a long series of reorganisations — even continuing today, apparently indefinitely.

It can be argued that the first major change at Cambridge after Nationalisation was not ill-conceived. The Chairman of the BTC's Eastern Area Board, Sir Reginald Wilson, wanted management to be more decentralised below Regional level and he instituted Line Traffic Managers for the Great Northern, the Great Eastern and the London, Tilbury & Southend components of the Eastern Region.

The first Line Managers too were well chosen; the brilliant Gerard Fiennes for the Great Northern was matched by the astute Willie Thorpe for the Great Eastern and John Dedman for the Tilbury. Cambridge saw the arrival of a Traffic Manager, responding to Thorpe at Line headquarters, who combined the functions of the former District Operating Superintendent, District Locomotive Running Superintendent and District Commercial Superintendent. The increased status of the Traffic Manager gave Cambridge a boost; a new office block near the station, named Great Eastern House, emphasised the BR presence.

Unfortunately, the fashion in organisations changed again and the Lines disappeared, being replaced by large geographical Divisions. Cambridge lost its Traffic Manager and was merged in the Norwich Division which, incidentally, involved a number of staff travelling daily to Norwich and back, some 136 miles by train. The new office block was disposed of not many years after it had been opened.

But the Divisions were not to be left undisturbed for very long. Reorganisation fever, stimulated by consultants scenting big fees, led to the commissioning of reports, one of which proposed a so-called Field Organisation replacing the six Regions with eight 'Territories'. Launched amid controversy and staff opposition, the 'Field' proposals involved a vast amount of detailed planning for their implementation, and much concern and confusion over the rôle of individuals. Cambridge staff looked unhappily to Norwich and Liverpool Street for guidance as to how they might be affected.

Finally, after nearly two years of discussion and argument, the 'Field' proposals were suddenly dropped, to general relief but also some recrimination over the waste of time and management effort.

A change that had meanwhile taken place was the amalgamation of the Eastern and North Eastern Regions and the removal of ER headquarters from Liverpool Street to York. Cambridge was now much further from the seat of Regional authority, and it was to be some time

*Above:* With wartime grime still sadly apparent, 'Claud' Class D15 No 2503 takes water on 15 April 1947. *H. C. Casserley*

*Below:* No 8866 takes water at Cambridge. *L. Hanson/The Gresley Society*

An elderly Class J65 0-6-0T, still with the shortened 'NE' on its tank sides, stands at Cambridge in 1947. *H. C. Casserley*

before the absurdity of overseeing the London commuter business from an office in Yorkshire was recognised.

After the collapse of 'Field', the next organisational phenomenon, around 1963, had been the rise of 'Area Management'. This had started as a simple economy drive in the budget for station-masters' salaries. It was plausibly argued that grouping several stations under a single manager would enable that official's status to be improved, and simultaneously show a reduction in the total salary bill. Any hidden costs in loss of staff morale and customer relations were not capable of being measured, though the removal of the local 'guv'nor', the visible boss on the spot, has had its drawbacks.

Topsy-ish, the functions of Area Managers 'just growed', being associated, in the search for economies, with the concept of two-tier instead of three-tier management. There was certainly an argument for some simplification, when one considers the drastic scaling-down of assets to be managed and staff numbers since Nationalisation. Cambridge emerged as an Area very similar geographically to a pre-Nationalisation District; but the Area Manager had neither the full supporting staff nor the standing of a former District Officer.

The end of the 1980s brought the creation of an Anglia Region, separate from the Eastern Region, and entirely divorced from York — a sensible if overdue measure. But the timing of the creation of Anglia was curious, since Sector management had already extended its empire to the point at which the demise of Regions seemed inevitable. Network SouthEast, the most effective empire-builder among the Sectors, by the spring of 1991 was able to announce that it would soon, in effect, virtually absorb the passenger businesses of both the Southern and Anglia Regions, and this was completed by April 1992, with the final disappearance of all Regional managements. Cambridge fell within the West Anglia sub-Sector; but the approaching shadow of privatisation meant that no organisation could be regarded as having any degree of permanency.

This was quickly proved to be the case after the passage of the Railways Act, 1993. The whole infrastructure of the Cambridge Line — stations, track, signalling — passed into the ownership of Railtrack, intended for sale to the private sector. Train services were now operated by three of the Train Operating Companies awaiting privatisation, namely West Anglia (for the Liverpool Street line, Great Northern (King's Cross services) and Regional Railways Central for the cross-country lines.

*Above:* Downham Market station prior to modernisation and electrification. *British Rail*

*Below:* Ely station prior to electrification. *Author's Collection*

# Modernisation: the First Phase

It can be argued that the two most important events affecting BR in the 30 years after Nationalisation were the Modernisation Plan of 1955 and the 'Re-Shaping' Report of 1963. Once the Government had approved in principle the investment proposals of the Modernisation Plan, and the changeover from steam to diesel and electric traction, the Eastern Region in 1956 set up a Planning Office under the General Manager to organise implementation within the Region. I was made head of this office, responsible to the Assistant General Manager, A.J. White.

Electrification and dieselisation were being planned simultaneously. The Region's management was strongly committed to electrification, initially for the London outer suburban area, though the East Coast main line remained an important long-term objective. (Suffice it to say that it was forced into second place behind the London Midland main line scheme, for reasons that it would not be appropriate to go into here.) Diesel traction would therefore have to be introduced on the main lines of the Region and also on those branch lines which were not within the London zone and earmarked for electrification.

The Liverpool Street Planning Office was concerned with translating the policy decisions of headquarters into plans that could be worked up into programmes of work by the big departments in the technical, engineering and operating functions. The Electrification Section was entrusted to a dedicated railwayman, John Bonham-Carter, who was eventually to crown a distinguished career as Chairman and General Manager of the London Midland Region. He had four schemes in hand at different stages of development — London, Tilbury & Southend; Shenfield to Southend Victoria; Shenfield to Colchester, Clacton and Walton; and 'Chenford'

(Liverpool Street to Chingford, Enfield, Hertford and Bishop's Stortford). With electrification over these routes progressing as fast as technical resources would permit, an intermediate diesel traction stage was clearly unnecessary; steam would stay until the 'sparks effect' took over.

The only electrification affecting the Cambridge line was 'Chenford'; though under it, Bishop's Stortford was not to be reached by the main line along the Lea Valley, but by reopening the Churchbury Loop (renamed Southbury) for passenger trains — a delayed revenge on London Transport, whose predecessor tramway company had forced the withdrawal of the rail passenger service 50 years previously. Modern building development now suggested that there was a worthwhile traffic potential. (Although the main line along the Lea Valley is slightly shorter, its stations are not generally in local centres, but sited on the edge of the built-up residential areas.) Reducing the total investment by postponing electrification of the Lea Valley section made the project a little more financially attractive.

The plan showed a certain cleverness typical of A.J. White. He was a very able man, with a fertile brain. He was a close friend of his General Manager, but he had a knack of rubbing people up the wrong way, partly because of his intolerance of other men's views. For example, if he was presiding over a meeting, he would go through the motions of asking others to speak; as soon as the invitation was taken up White would imply that this was a waste of time. He would take off his jacket, or get up from his chair and open or close a window, or adjust the heating. His body language was quite unmistakable!

It was a pity that closing the gap along the main line had to wait until 1967. Meanwhile the

*Above:* Early diesel power on the line is represented by No D5302, which later migrated to Scotland, seen on a Cambridge–King's Lynn train on 13 June 1959. *E.R. Wethersett/Ian Allan Library*

*Below:* A sad sight: Hunstanton station, awaiting closure, is unstaffed and served by a shuttle DMU service to King's Lynn only, in June 1967. *R. F. Roberts*

growing number of commuters from Bishop's Stortford had to make do with a stopping electric service, apart from the less frequent long-distance trains. The best of these, too, began to make their first stop at Audley End, where the car park had started to fill up with commuters living in the pleasant countryside of north-east Hertfordshire and north-west Essex.

Bishop's Stortford passengers did however reap the benefit of a station modernisation scheme with a facelift restoring the original quite attractive building, while the track layout and signalling were modified to improve speed for non-stopping trains; stabling sidings were added for electric stock. Other improvements included the recovery and restoration of the three stations on the Southbury Loop and — later — a connection at Tottenham to the Victoria Line tube.

'Chenford' opened in November 1960. In one respect, White's planning had an unfortunate result, in the design of the rolling stock.

The London & North Eastern Railway had planned the electrification from Liverpool Street to Shenfield, which had been brought into service after Nationalisation, in 1949, with power-door open saloon coaches. White, however, was averse to following where others had led and decided that slam-door compartment stock would offer the greatest number of seats for any given floor area, and also the quickest times of entraining and detraining at station stops. He told the ex-LNER officers that they should follow Southern Railway (and Southern Region) practice.

I argued strongly that slam-door stock was obsolete: it was draughty (droplights being frequently left down in winter) and often a cause of accidents. Doors left unclosed caused delays. The compartment design was also outmoded. In this I was supported by that stalwart railwayman Harold Few, District Operating Superintendent,

Hackney Downs station pictured at the 'Chenford' electrification scheme of 1960. *Author's Collection*

Stratford and later Assistant General Manager, (Movements). However, White used the General Manager's authority to overrule us, and in consequence commuters into Liverpool Street were saddled, like those on the Southern, with electric stock built to an obsolete design, which had to last for thirty years. (Rolling stock with power doors finally arrived in the 1980s.)

Apart from the design of rolling stock, a problem of electrification systems had arisen. The Chief Electrical Engineer at BR headquarters, S.B. Warder, had come to the conclusion that, apart from the Southern Region where third-rail dc should continue to be employed, future electrification should be on the 50-cycles 25kV ac overhead system first tried out on the London Midland Region. This presented the Eastern Region with a problem. It had just completed two lines (Manchester–Sheffield–Wath and Liverpool Street–Shenfield) on the 1500V dc overhead system. Planning was well advanced for extending this on all the four new schemes under way. Some contracts had been placed and quite appreciable cost would be incurred in a changeover.

I argued that the networks based on Liverpool Street and Fenchurch Street were self-contained, and problems of compatability with other routes would not arise if 1,500V dc were extended all over them. This well-tried technology could be confidently employed on the basis of experience. Costs would be lower, completion would be sooner, interference with traffic minimised, and teething troubles avoided. There was no reason to believe that the dc overhead system could not meet all traffic demands.

However, A.J. White, always attracted by what seemed the less orthodox solution, persuaded the General Manager C. K. Bird that ac and high voltage was the system of the future. At a top-level meeting with the BTC, C.K. Bird when asked for his view replied 'I would not want the Eastern Region to be excluded from the most advanced technology'. So, on the turn of a phrase, the decision was taken.

Implementing it was a heavy and expensive task, especially so far as obtaining clearance was concerned. That was not all: problems with the traction equipment appeared, to such an extent that, half-way through, serious consideration was given to reversing the policy and reverting to 1,500V dc. John Bonham-Carter prepared a paper objectively setting out the consideration and the financial effects. After some heart-searching, it was decided to persevere with 25kV ac. This involved converting the 1,500V dc system already in use to ac after less than a dozen years in service, to permit flexibility in working rolling stock.

It was decided to reduce the engineering work required to obtain the overhead clearances needed for 25kV by adopting 6.25kV in the built-up area, although it was later established that this was not necessary as lesser clearances were electrically safe.

When services started with ac trains to Bishop's Stortford, and the rest of the 'Chenford' services, problems were experienced with traction motors, transformers and rectifiers, which led to all trains in turn having to be withdrawn for a time for modification. Eventually the troubles were overcome.

The diesel traction section of the Planning Office was in the charge of H.R. (Ray) Gomersall, who had been trained as a steam locomotive running man under the formidable L.P. Parker, a martinet of whom R.H.N. Hardy has given a vivid portrait. Parker, however, recognised brains in his young men, and Ray Gomersall was clever as well as a dedicated railwayman: from being a craft apprentice he had risen very quickly largely thanks to grooming and tuition from Parker. He was however perhaps too readily attracted by the new and the unorthodox, a characteristic he shared with A.J. White. But he had the knack of persuasiveness in whatever case he was arguing at the moment.

He changed from a steam man to a diesel proponent easily, unlike many of his contemporaries. The types of diesel multiple-unit for local services and diesel locomotives for long-distance trains were basically determined at BR headquarters, though Regional requirements as regards power, and preferences as between designs, including seating, were taken into account. The main activity of the Planning Office on the diesel side therefore was designing maintenance facilities and preserving essential liaison between top management and the technical departments.

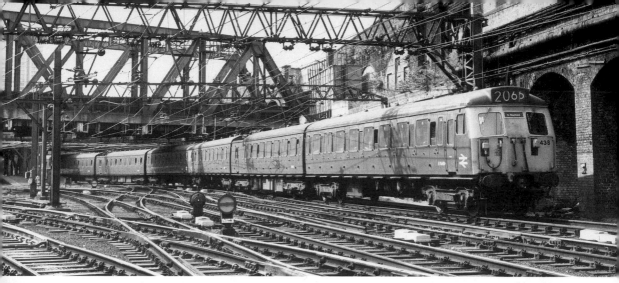

*Above:* Two Class 305 EMUs depart from Liverpool Street on 10 September 1977 with the 12.43 service to Bishop's *Stortford. Brian Morrison*

*Left:* Brush-built Class 31/1 No 31314 takes the 11.30 service from King's Lynn through Bethnal Green on 8 December 1979. *Brian Morrison*

*Below left:* Class 37 No 37025 stops at Audley End with a Cambridge train on 1 June 1981. *Brian Morrison*

*Above right:* Class 47/4 No 47634 provides the power for the 17.35 train from Cambridge as it heads into Bishop's Stortford on 16 August 1986. *R. F. Roberts*

*Right:* Class 47 No 47160 passes Whittlesford with the 13.30 service from King's Lynn on 1 June 1981. *Brian Morrison*

Class 37 No 37039 heads the 13.36 service towards Whittlesford on 1 June 1981. *Brian Morrison*

*Top:* The 17.35 King's Lynn–Liverpool Street train arrives at Ely on 15 July 1987 behind Class 47/4 No 47634 *Henry Ford*. *Brian Morrison*

*Above:* The 15.00 King's Lynn–Liverpool Street express passes Littleport on 15 July 1987, headed by Class 47/4 No 47573 *The London Standard* in the first version of the Network SouthEast Sector livery. *Brian Morrison*

*Left:* Class 47/4 No 47583 *County Of Hertfordshire* slows for the scheduled Ely stop on 15 July 1987 with the 16.35 Liverpool Street–King's Lynn 'Fenman' service. A Class 101 DMU and withdrawn and stored 'Hastings' DEMUs are in the sidings. *Brian Morrison*

*Below left:* The 14.35 Liverpool Street–King's Lynn service is whisked past the ancient-looking crossing keeper's hut at Snipes Lane, Wormley, on 16 September 1987, powered by Class 86/2 No 86205 *City of Lancaster*. At this date the train would have been hauled by a Class 47 north of Cambridge. *Brian Morrison*

*Below:* On 23 March 1988 Class 86/2 No 86259 *Peter Pan*, with the 15.35 Liverpool Street–Cambridge service, meets Class 310 EMU No 310085, with the 14.25 Cambridge–Liverpool Street train, near Coppermill Junction, Clapton. *Brian Morrison*

145

The first through electric service train from King's Lynn to King's Cross on 24 August 1990 was entitled the 'Fenman' — a title first conferred on a Liverpool Street–King's Lynn/Hunstanton service in the 1949 summer timetable. *Brian Morrison*

Class 59 No 59002 *Yeoman Enterprise* is pictured at the Foster Yeoman depot at Harlow Mill on 16 September 1987. *Brian Morrison*

*Above:* In Civil Engineer's livery, Class 31/5 No 31541 heads an engineers' train at King's Lynn on 29 September 1990. This was just one of a number of exhibits at the station in connection with the West Anglia Gala Day.
*Brian Morrison*

*Below:* The first catenary mast for the electrification from Cambridge having been ceremonially sunk at King's Lynn on 30 August 1989, a special train for guests and dignitaries travelled along the route being electrified to Cambridge. The train is seen at Downham Market having made a photo-stop. The all-NSE stock is headed by an immaculate Class 47/4 No 47581 *Great Eastern*. *Brian Morrison*

*Left:* The original office block at Bishop's Stortford viewed from the road. *Author*

*Centre left:* Bishop's Stortford station in 1992 — the new Travel Centre stands beside the original station. *Author*

*Bottom left:* The exterior of the remodelled Ely station seen in 1992. *Author*

*Right:* One hundred and fifty years ago this location at Stratford was the point where the Eastern Counties met the Northern & Eastern; today it still sees services, now electrified, diverging to the north. *Author's Collection*

*Bottom right:* Formed by Class 317/1 No 317348, a down service from King's Cross is pictured on arrival at King's Lynn. *Author*

*Above:* The down platform at Ely pictured following the completion of the station's remodelling in 1992. *Author*

*Left:* The exterior of King's Lynn station, 1992. *Author*

*Bottom left:* The end of the line; a view of the buffer stops at King's Lynn taken in 1992. *Author*

# Modernisation:
# The Final Phase

After the completion of 'Chenford' in 1960, electrification hung fire for a while. By 1978 however the second stage of the Great Northern suburban electrification brought the wires all the way to Royston, only 13 miles short of Cambridge. Stopping at Royston seemed a case of spoiling the ship for want of a ha'p'orth of tar. The real reason was probably that if this gap was closed, the Department of Transport would argue that there was no case for electrifying the Great Eastern line between Bishop's Stortford and Cambridge. For a decade, therefore, King's Cross semi-fast electrics ran only to Royston, whence an hourly two-car DMU carried passengers on to Cambridge, alternate trains being non-stop and all stations.

Eventually in 1987 authority was given to extend the wires from Bishop's Stortford to Cambridge. While the work was in progress there were some curious procedures on Sundays when the engineers required full line possessions. I have a vivid memory of leaving Liverpool Street in a diesel locomotive-hauled train which proceeded first to Stratford and then took the Channelsea curve to reach the North London line which enabled it to arrive, via Canonbury, at Finsbury Park. It then stood for a considerable time before the Great Northern system could recover from its surprise at such a visitor from the Great Eastern and allow it to continue on a course that had been announced at Liverpool Street as 'non-stop to Cambridge'. The controller at the panel however gave precedence to a stopping train all the way to Hitchin!

Almost at the same time, authority was given to close the gap between Royston and the now electrified GE line at Shepreth Junction (Shelford), merely 10 more miles of wiring. This led to the institution of fast King's

Cross–Cambridge trains, though the Class 317 four-car units were lacking in the creature comforts of the 'Beer Trains' despite their 100mph speed capacity.

Pending electrification to King's Lynn, interim timetables were in force in 1990 and 1991 following withdrawal of the diesel locomotive-hauled trains. While the Liverpool Street–Cambridge trains became Class 317 multiple-units the remaining through Liverpool Street to King's Lynn trains were hauled on the same principle as the Liverpool Street–Norwich expresses while the wires extended no further than Ipswich. Electric locomotives performed the first leg of the journey, and Class 47 diesels the remainder — a very unsatisfactory arrangement from the aspect of utilisation. On the Cambridge line elderly Class 86 electric locomotives, cascaded from elsewhere, were paired with the diesels.

Apart from the few through services, it was necessary to change at Cambridge into DMU sets which took 59 min for the $41\frac{1}{4}$ miles.

Memory recalls many dismally slow journeys to and from Cambridge on the 'day of rest', even in summer when visitors (largely American, perhaps descendants of the 'foreigners and other unseemly persons' whom Dr Corrie execrated in 1851) seek to visit the ancient university and bring revenue into the railway coffers.

Amends were however finally made in 1992, when the wires reached King's Lynn, and revolutionary changes were made to the service over what BR provisionally designated the Fen Line. King's Cross had already become the prime London terminus for Cambridge, with its 'clock-face' service and sole intermediate stop at Stevenage; now an hourly King's Cross–King's Lynn service was instituted reaching Cambridge with the single Stevenage stop in 57min. In 1994 an even more revolutionary change appeared; Cambridge gained a non-stop train every half-hour, with a journey time of 52min, alternate trains being extended to King's Lynn, with minor variations in the morning and evening peak hours. Class 317 sets were used, but the trolley catering service was withdrawn as was the short-lived naming of one service the 'Fenman'.

The southern part of the Cambridge line has benefited from the opening of the short branch, making a triangular junction with the main line just north of Stansted Station (now rejoicing in its full title of Stansted Mountfitchet). This leads, through a short tunnel under the runway, into a new rail terminus at Stansted Airport. Airport trains, composed of four-car Class 322 units, run every half-hour to and from Liverpool Street, throughout the day. Originally the only interme-diate stop was at Tottenham Hale, to provide interconnection with London Underground's Victoria Line, but some Bishop's Stortford stops were added later. For a time the cross-country services into Cambridge from the Midlands were extended into the airport via the north spur but lack of patronage over this final link in the jour-ney led to its withdrawal.

The balance sheet produced by electrification shows many gainers and some losers. King's Lynn, Ely and Cambridge enjoy a fast (up to 100mph south of Hitchin) and frequent service to and from King's Cross — next door to what the Great Eastern loved to call its 'West End' ter-minus. But 'City gents', with offices within the Square Mile, commuting from Cambridge or Audley End, have lost the comfortable if rather leisurely non-stop trains, with buffet cars, into Liverpool Street; even in the peak hours the new electrics call at Whittlesford, Audley End, Bishop's Stortford, Harlow Town and Tottenham. Cambridge commuters in short have to balance the excellence of the King's Cross ser-vice against losses elsewhere; but the well-heeled commuters who fill the car park at Audley End in particular, may have regrets.

*Below:* Class 315 No 315860 and Class 322 No 322484 make scheduled stops at the new-look Tottenham Hale station on 19 March 1992. The trains form the 10.56 Broxbourne–Stratford and 11.00 Liverpool Street–Stansted Airport services respectively. *Brian Morrison*

*Above right:* The interior of the new Tottenham Hale sta-tion seen looking northwards. *Author*

*Below right:* The south end of Bishop's Stortford station pictured in 1992. *Author*

*Above:* A 'Stansted Express' bound for Liverpool Street approaches Bishop's Stortford formed of Class 322 EMU No 322482. *Author*

*Left:* Bishop's Stortford station in 1992; the photograph shows the staggering of the platforms and the track, on the far right, once used by the Dunmow and Braintree trains.
*Author*

*Bottom left:* A driver's eye view of the approach to the new terminus at Stansted Airport.
*Author*

*Above right:* To inaugurate rail links with Stansted Airport, special trains were run from Liverpool Street and Peterborough to the new station on 29 January 1991. On arrival at Stansted are Class 322 No 322481 and Class 158 No 158755.
*Brian Morrison*

*Right:* Class 317/1 No 317318 enters Bishop's Stortford station on 4 December 1992 forming the 11.58 service from Cambridge to Liverpool Street.
*Brian Morrison*

15

# The Line Remembered

It might be thought that travelling in a stop-ping, or at best semi-fast, electric Class 317 or 321 unit has removed all, or nearly all, the interest from a journey along the Cambridge main line. That is not so for anyone with a feeling for railway history or railway archaeology.

Starting at Liverpool Street, the rebuilt station has miraculously preserved and even extended Wilson's splendid train shed. In its fresh colour-ing and clear glass it can be appreciated in a totally different way to when it was a mysterious cavern full of drifting steam and smoke, echoing to the panting of Westinghouse pumps.

Departing, the chances are that the Cambridge train will snake its way into the 'cel-lars' whence through openings some vestiges of Bishopsgate Low Level platforms can still be glimpsed. Nipping rapidly up the Bethnal Green incline recalls spectacular pictures from Great Eastern Railway days, of descending trains cross-ing on the bank with those climbing towards Bethnal Green shooting columns of smoke over the East End.

The double crossover just beyond the curve at Bethnal Green, linking the Fast and Slow Hackney Downs lines, replaces one formerly sited in the middle of the curve. Having regard to the already sharp radius of the curve, the crossover bore hard on wheel-flanges and was difficult for the engineers to maintain.

The track geometry between Bethnal Green and Hackney Downs is not of the kind that Brunel or Robert Stephenson would have approved: the line, entirely on viaduct, shows odd kinks due to constraints in laying it out through a closely developed area in the second half of the 19th century. Although the line speed is restricted here, no less a person than the Earl of Athlone (Queen Mary's brother), once wrote to complain he had been thrown to the floor by the train's rough riding.

After Hackney Downs and before Clapton, between the short tunnels, there was formerly a station known as Queen's Road; no traces of the platforms can now be seen. At Clapton Junction one may wonder why no move was ever made to realign the track and raise the permissible speed for Cambridge expresses; instead, the Chingford locals have the unrestricted run.

The view over the Walthamstow Marshes, with Clapton Terrace and the Lea, is striking. The marshes themselves, less than four miles from the centre of the City of London, are green, empty and deserted except for plant life and the occasional abandoned rusty motorcar.

From Copper Mill Junction the former inde-pendent goods lines can just be traced; they were busy when there was heavy freight passing between Whitemoor and Temple Mills. Their for-mation has now been partly built over. The spur to the Tottenham & Hampstead line remains, but the subsidiary spur formerly used by St Pancras–Cambridge trains has been dismantled.

Tottenham Hale station obtained new impor-tance when it became an inter-change point with London Underground's Victoria Line. From a local traffic point of view its site is less advanta-geous than would have been the position nearer to High Cross proposed in the days of the Northern & Eastern. Its current striking moderni-sation is fully justified by the number of Cambridge trains and 'Stansted Expresses' booked to call there.

Passing Northumberland Park (originally called Marsh Lane, then just Park, for a time) the former big gasworks used to require a succession of coal trains congesting the main line on their way into and out of sidings.

At Angel Road the original branch to Enfield, disused for passenger trains since the opening of the Hackney Downs–Seven Sisters route, can no longer be traced. Between Angel Road and Ponder's End there formerly stood an important signalbox at Pickett's Lock, controlling the movement of freight trains on to and off the passenger lines. Ponder's End is unremarkable apart from having delighted Charles Lamb: 'beautiful name, how emblematic', he wrote.

At Cheshunt, one of the Lea Valley stations rebuilt by the GER in its substantial style, now simplified, the Southbury Loop trains terminating use a bay platform on the down side. The long section from Cheshunt to Broxbourne was formerly broken by an intermediate block post at Wormley. Broxbourne station was rebuilt on a slightly different site at the time of the 'Chenford' electrification. The views of the river, with boat moorings on the up side and the Church and meadow on the down side, are delightful. On the up side there is still a small yard formerly used for holding freight trains. At Broxbourne Junction, the Hertford East line curves away sharply near a 'Go-Kart' racetrack at Rye House.

Sadly for British Rail's traffic, the big power station which used to demand service from coal trains, is no more. Immediately after the junction the Cambridge line crosses the Lea by a rather handsome girder bridge. Roydon, the next station, had an attractive former station-house converted to private use. On the east side of the line the canalised River Stort is charming.

Harlow Town Station, also rebuilt in connection with electrification, replaces a former rather attractive countrified station called Burnt Mill. Harlow New Town is sited to the West of the old village, and the former Harlow station is now designated Harlow Mill.

Mills are in fact a feature of this part of England where even slow-moving streams such as the Lea and the Stort have been made to work hard. Buildings at the next station, Sawbridgeworth, remind us of this. Between Sawbridgeworth and Bishop's Stortford the disused signalbox at Spellbrook, where there used to be the freight loop, still stands.

Bishop's Stortford, with the original station block externally restored in 1960, and its platform awning supported by columns with capitals picked out in colour, has lost some of the former importance it held when it was a regular stopping place for Cambridge line expresses to Norwich and Hunstanton. Leaving the station, while the main line is level for a short distance, the bank up which the branch trains for Dunmow and Braintree used to travel can just be distinguished. Their former trackbed curves away to the east and is lost among gardens and buildings.

Soon after Bishop's Stortford the line, which has been on very slightly rising grades almost all the way from Bethnal Green, begins the short but relatively steep ascent from Stansted to the summit at Elsenham. The curve through Stansted (as the station is universally still called, rather than Stansted Mountfitchet) makes the signal for the Airport line junction difficult for drivers to read well in advance. The Airport branch leaves to the east and forms one side of a triangle.

The Airport line, just over three miles long, becomes single before entering a short tunnel under the runway. Emerging, it curves and climbs into the Airport station which has three platforms served by the dedicated 'Stansted Express' stock in green and cream livery providing a half-hourly service from and to Liverpool Street.

The curves approaching Elsenham are severe, around the headwaters of the River Cam or Granta. Elsenham station is the most 'truly rural' on the line, and has preserved a charming Great Eastern character; its timber building on the up platform has a projecting awning supported by decorative cast-iron columns. The platforms are staggered, which adds to the interest. No clear trace of the Elsenham and Thaxted Light Railway can be seen on the up side.

On the downhill stretch to Newport, steam-hauled trains used to reach their maximum speed, though, if they were stopping at Audley End, this was short-lived. The beautiful and historic timbered houses on the road beside the railway overbridge are glimpsed only momentarily from the train. The legend that one of them was used to lodge Nell Gwynne when King Charles II was going racing at Newmarket is amusing if doubtful. Audley End station (at Wendens Ambo village), now well restored, is a little gem by the architect Francis Thompson, with verandahs and round-headed windows as well as the *porte-cochère* mentioned in Chapter 2. The modern 'conservatory' type of waiting room on the up platform consorts reasonably well with the original building. The branch for Saffron Walden has been obliterated.

The Braybrooke coat of arms that adorns the tunnel portal at Littlebury is unseen by the passenger. The two tunnels mark the beginning of the 12-mile downhill stretch to Cambridge. At Great Chesterford virtually no trace remains of the formation of the Newmarket Railway. The freight loops at this minor summit of the line have been curtailed. The attractive building on the up side is to a design that Francis Thompson also used on the Chester & Holyhead Railway. It has been converted under private ownership into a wine bar and restaurant. A little further, at Duxford Mill, on the down side a splendid private garden, sometimes open to the public, can be glimpsed and is of interest at all times of the year.

Shelford shows little sign of its former importance as the junction for the line to Sudbury and Mark's Tey, but trackbed of the branch can be traced for some little distance. Just past Shelford station the Great Northern line from Royston joins the main line at Shepreth Junction with a curve that is of short enough radius to impose a severe speed restriction. A couple of miles further comes the bridge carrying Long Road over the railway, with the now disused arch 150yd to the west through which the London & North Western line reached Cambridge via such exotically named places as Gamlingay, Old North Road and Lord's Bridge (the 'station without a village').

It is odd to reflect that even as recently as the beginning of the 1960s Cambridge was envisaged as a nodal point on the strategic freight route (Didcot–Oxford–Bletchley–Cambridge) intended to relieve the congested London area, and justifying the massive concrete flyover at Bletchley which stands useless today.

The home signal for Cambridge station marks a spot where the signalmen used to bring almost every down train to a halt before deciding to admit it to a platform line. The long-standing custom of passing down trains to the north end of the long platform via the scissors crossover meant that knowledgeable travellers would walk to the rear of the train approaching Cambridge, to reduce the distance to the exit gate after alighting. Occasionally, however without warning, a down train might be diverted to the south end of the platform, to the discomfiture of the regulars.

Cambridge station yard has always been well supplied with taxis, partly because of the uncertainties of the bus service, whether the former green Ortona, the red Eastern National or the blue and white Cambus vehicles of to-day. However, the user of public transport may reflect that at long last Cambridge has an hourly service to London in 56min — and that to King's Cross, which Heads of Houses considered less plebeian than Liverpool Street.

Even so, I remember with regret a Hunstanton–Liverpool Street express of 1939 with its Holden '1500' 4-6-0, and its warm, well-lit restaurant car offering three- and four-course meals on clean tablecloths and cutlery still marked 'GER'. Cambridge may be reconciled to becoming merely a Great Northern appendage — and Edmund Denison's ghost may be smiling grimly. But ghosts of Great Eastern men — above all Henry Thornton's — will be glowering.

A former Eastern Counties Railway four-wheel coach was attached to the Stratford Works shunter, No 7230, at an 'Open Day' at Ilford in 1937. *T. Middlemass*

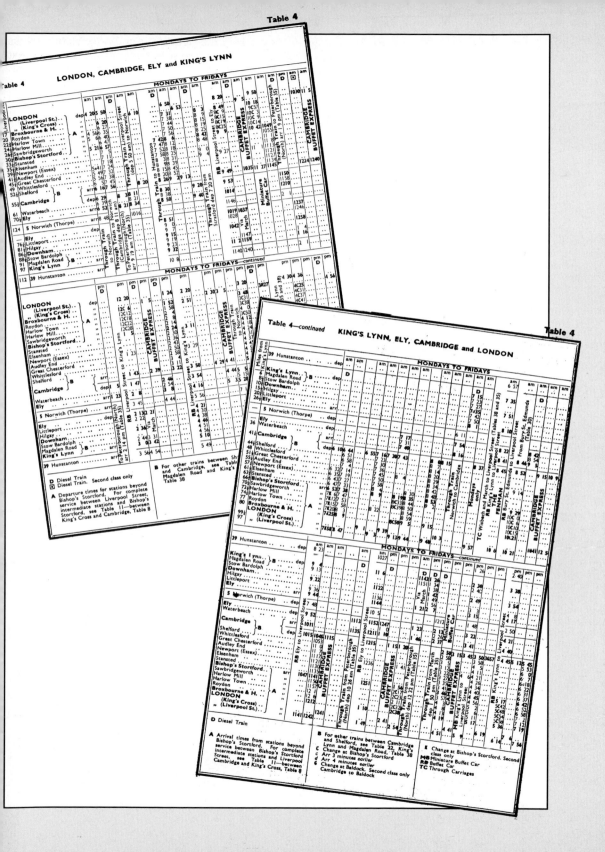

'E4' 2-4-0 No 62785 — the last 2-4-0 in service in Britain — leaves Cambridge for the Colchester line on 3 May 1959. This was the last day in service for the locomotive.
*J.C. Beckett*